Cheap Psychological Tricks for Parents

62 Sure-fire Secrets and Solutions for Successful Parenting

Perry W. Buffington, Ph.D.

Illustrated by

Jen Singh

PEACHTREE
ATLANTA

Published by
PEACHTREE PUBLISHERS LTD.
1700 Chattahoochee Avenue
Atlanta, Georgia 30318-2112

www.peachtree-online.com

Text © 2003 by Perry Buffington, Ph.D.
Cover and interior illustrations © 2003 by Jen Singh

Book and cover design by Loraine M. Joyner
Book composition by Melanie M. McMahon

Manufactured in the United States of America

10 9 8 7 6 5 4 3 2 1
First Edition

Library of Congress Cataloging-in-Publication Data

Buffington, Perry W.
    Cheap psychological tricks for parents / written by Perry W.
Buffington ; illustrated by Jen Singh.-- 1st ed.
        p. cm.
Includes bibliographical references.
    ISBN 1-56145-204-1
    1. Parenting--Psychological aspects. 2. Child rearing--Psychological
aspects. 3. Parent and child--Psychological aspects. I. Title.
    HQ755.8 .B84 2003
    649'.1--dc21   2002015654

Table of Contents

Part III: THE BODY

Part IV: THE BRAIN

Part V: THE HEART

"I now have a seven-year-old boy and a nine-year-old boy, so all I can say is, 'I apologize.'"

—MATT GROENING, CREATOR OF THE SIMPSONS

Introduction

Think back to the good old days of *Leave It to Beaver, The Andy Griffith Show,* and *Father Knows Best*—even *The Brady Bunch*. Those were the days when parents were parents, and the kids knew it. Then something happened. Somehow, in the 1970s, the focus in parenting changed from "parents as parents" to "parents as teachers." Teaching is a function of parenting, but there's a lot more to it than that. As expected, this parents-as-teachers movement didn't quite produce the desired results. Some say it failed. A bigger failure, however, is the new trend in parenting that followed.

In the 1980s, some well-meaning advocates of permissiveness suggested that parents should be their children's friends. This approach required modern parents to give up many of the principles that the parents of previous generations had stood for. Friendly parents, it was thought, would be perfect parents. Unfortunately, the powers promoting this new approach forgot that children do not think or act like adults. They also forgot that children must have structure *and* discipline *and* limits. They erroneously concluded that parents could buy their child's good behavior. As a result, many of that decade's children developed an identity based on things.

Good old-fashioned ethics, morals, educational pursuits, religion, and other significant issues were neither in vogue nor thought to be important.

By the early 1990s, some parents were seeing the fruits of this "improved" friendly technique. Their children were out-of-control, had no understanding of who they were, and were living in the "endless instant." Something had to give.

Today, many parents have rediscovered what yesterday's parents knew. It's important for parents to teach. It's certainly important for parents to be friends with their children. But it's more important for parents to be parents and lead their children. As a result, the latest trend in parenting is based on an old philosophy that has worked for thousands of years. For parents to be effective, they must be leaders, exerting responsible power over their children.

Parents as leaders—what a deceptively simple, and magnificent, time-honored concept. So many parenting books have touched on the issue, but few have spelled it out. This book delineates these "leading" techniques via cheap psychological tricks you can use to become a loving "general of your household." These tricks are designed to help you marshal your troops.

Ahead of you are sixty-two cheap psychological tricks. Each trick is based in sound psychological/

behavioral practice that will get you up and running, leading your children, teaching them how to solve problems, and preparing them for their brave new world. If that's not enough motivation, think of it this way. You're not just leading your children; indirectly, you're leading your children's children and successive generations. So, with that daunting task, good luck! Your family (and generations to come) is depending on you.

Dr. Buff

ᎮᏗᏒᎢ I

THE BIG PICTURE

"Children have never been very good at listening to their elders, but they have never failed to imitate them."

—JAMES BALDWIN

Cheap Trick No. 1

What's in a Name?

Rumor has it that a rose by any other name would smell as sweet, but that may not be true when it comes to children's names. It's time to take a lesson from the Bamana people of Mali. According to custom, they name their children after respected elders in the community. As a result, the children are encouraged to and often do take on the attributes of their namesakes. Actually, they even take this naming process a step further. Say a child is named after his grandfather. The father of the child will address his child as "father." While this may sound quaint, there's actually a wonderful cheap psychological trick hiding in this child-naming tradition.

Many parents-to-be make it a point to purchase a book that lists baby names and their meanings. The only problem is that other people—unless they have also read the book—don't know what the names mean. Jason may mean "strong" and Andrea "spirited," but these esoteric meanings are unfamiliar to most of the world. Instead of looking for a unique or different sounding name, perhaps you should find a namesake for your child. Do you want your child to grow up big and strong like his father, Patrick? Then maybe Patrick Jr. or Patrick III is in order. If your grandmother is highly respected and revered in the community, you might want to name your child after her. People often believe that namesakes have the attributes of the individuals for whom they are named. Naming children after someone in the family who is loved and admired gives them a leg up in the community.

There are some peculiar, perhaps even perverse, twists to this namesake rule. Naming a child for a celebrity does not guarantee that she will take on the attributes of that celebrity. Celebrity names tend to be short-lived and fad-driven. Celebrity names like Britney, for instance—don't take offense, this is a teaching example—may sound appropriate today, but as time passes, they may become dated and embarrassing. If you're genuinely interested in naming a child after a celebrity, pick a well-known person with admirable qualities who has left a significant legacy. Names like Martin, Abraham, Theresa, Mary, or Eleanor have a substantive ring because they're associated with people of integrity.

Finally, be aware of the child's initials. For example, Arthur Seymour Sullivan, well-known composer and the Sullivan in Gilbert & Sullivan, probably avoided monogrammed shirts.

What's the cheap psychological trick? Choose your child's name carefully, so she can aspire to be someone of stature, rather than a has-been pop star. Look for namesakes in your family or heritage who may set an example for your child and communicate positive things about her to your community.

REFERENCE

Arnoldi, M. J. "The Legacy of a Name among the Bamana of Mali." In A. Cohn and L. Leach (Eds.), *Generations: A Universal Family Album*. New York: Pantheon Books, 1987.

Cheap Trick No. 2

KidThink

Believe it or not, kids don't think like adults. You may be saying, "Duh!" but your actions tell a different tale. Most parents are easily lulled into believing that their children think just like them. Not so. Not even possible. Even the most seemingly mature child is still precisely that—a child. Long after they've developed physical maturity, children are still working on emotional maturity. There are actually four specific stages of thinking that separate children from adults.

Stage 1—Sensorimotor, age zero to two. It's a fancy psychological word, and it means that most of a child's "thinking" centers on his senses and motor development. If you want to influence children in this phase, do it through their senses.

Stage 2—Pre-operational, ages two to seven. From "terrible twos" to first-grade jitters, a child's thinking is me-centered, and you're just an ancillary part of that thought process. He thinks only from his perspective, which is why sharing is so difficult. Don't try to force your logical thinking on him; it will be lost.

Stage 3—Concrete operational, ages seven to twelve. At this point, a child's thinking becomes far more logical, but he still thinks like a child. This stage tricks adults. Parents think their little boy is becoming a little man. They're wrong. This is the stage where your actions speak far louder to your child than your words. In fact, many parents learn about now that their words seem to go in their child's left ear, rumble around a bit, and then come out the right ear. Don't be surprised if your child, even as he approaches ages eleven, has difficulty interpreting what's real and what's not. Remember, they haven't mastered adult thinking yet.

Stage 4—Formal operational, ages twelve and up. If logical thinking is ever going to kick in, it'll happen about now. Moreover, your young adult can deal with abstract concepts like love, friendship, and loyalty. The problem is that many children never master anything more than rudimentary abstract thinking. As a result, it's estimated by many researchers that 50 percent of the population is stuck in the concrete stage three. This explains the tone of political commercials and mindless television sitcoms.

What's the cheap psychological trick? Understand where your child is developmentally. Talk to him using logic he can understand. If you want your child to grow intellectually, communicate with him in a manner that is effective for his current stage. Children do not think like adults, but maybe— after twelve years of your tutoring— they'll start to get the basics of adult logic.

REFERENCE

Piaget, J. *The Origins of Intelligence in Children.* New York: W. W. Norton, 1963.

Cheap Trick No. 3

What Do I Tell the Children?

On September 11, 2001, the two World Trade Center towers were savagely destroyed and thousands died. On that day, every parent wondered: "What do I tell my children?" Sadly, events in our world often require parents to have difficult conversations with their children. Here are guidelines that you can use should the need arise. The answers are as easy to remember as the alphabet.

A—Age Appropriate. When explaining a traumatic or difficult event to a child, remember to use age-appropriate language. It's important to explain that a bad event is real. Even children as old as twelve often have difficulty distinguishing between real and imagined. If they're watching live footage on television, it may look no different to them than a PG-13 movie.

Explain a traumatic event in real, age-appropriate terms but don't embellish the events with gory details.

B—Be Honest. Young children can easily understand that there are evil or mean people in the world; you don't need to make up an explanation for the behavior of evildoers. If you're explaining a death, tell your child the truth instead of saying, "Grandma's asleep." Even if you're trying to protect your child, using this explanation could prompt him to fear sleep. Believe it or not, children can understand at an early age the concept of death. In fact, its finality may be easier for them to understand than divorce.

C—Consistent Routine. After the unconditional love of their parents, consistent routine is the most important factor in a child's life. As quickly as possible after any traumatic event, return your child to his usual daily schedule so that his life feels in control and secure.

D—Delete TV. Remember that 90 percent of what children learn comes through their eyes; too much uncensored visual stimulation can exacerbate any trauma. If you need to keep up with current events as they unfold, watch news updates while your child is playing outside, sleeping, or away from the house. The newspaper is often a better source for difficult news, even for adults; television images, which seem more real and visceral, can create more pain.

E—Express Positive Emotions and Actions. Express your love. When children feel threatened, they need to feel loved and protected. Make sure to tell your child frequently that you love him. Express caring for others who are suffering. It's good for your child to witness this. Action is a powerful healing agent. Explaining to your child that you're donating blood after a catastrophe demonstrates to him that you're doing your part. Ask your child what he would like to do to help out. He may feel better if he feels he can take action. And finally, express your faith. Use it to help you and your family navigate through troubled times. This will give your child a clearer idea of the role of faith in a lifetime.

What's the cheap psychological trick? Use the alphabet approach to negotiate a difficult conversation. When you speak with your child about a traumatic event, honesty and caring expressed in age-appropriate language works best.

REFERENCE

Schneider, M. F. *Help! My Teacher Hates Me.* New York: Workman Publishing, 1994.

Cheap Trick No. 4

Halo or Horns?

Remember the old saying, "Be careful what you wish for"? Well, it applies to parenting. Experts typically refer to this phenomenon as "halo or horns," "self-fulfilling prophecies," or even "experimenter bias." This means that if you expect your child to be a good child, you may put out signals that help create that very result. On the other hand, if you expect your child to be a little devil, you behave—perhaps subconsciously—in a way that is likely to create a child who misbehaves.

Many parents are afraid that their children will become problematic when they hit adolescence. The media, society, even schools perpetuate this myth. It may or may not happen. Nevertheless, most parents don't even realize that their parenting approach changes when puberty hits. They may become more critical and challenging and less trusting. Their fears and doubts are communicated both subtly and clearly in their speech, behavior, and expressions of emotion. Be careful: If you expect horns, you may get them—and all because you were afraid of them in the first place.

What about halos? Same thing. Parents who expect their children to be good typically rear good children. As a result, they don't overcorrect, overwatch, or overcriticize. They know how to praise their children when they're being good. Unfortunately, most parents only respond to their children when they are bad. As a result, some children are ignored when they are good.

What's the cheap psychological trick? Parenting is the art of positive direction. You get the child you expect, so show your child how to be good. Then expect your child to be good, and she'll most likely meet your expectations. Make it a point to notice and to reward your child when she is good, and you'll find that the little devil has no need to come out and play.

REFERENCE

Goldstein, M. D., J. R. Hopkins, and M. J. Strube. "The Eye of the Beholder: A Classroom Demonstration of Observer Bias." *Teaching of Psychology* 21 (1994): 154–157.

Cheap Trick No. 5

High School Glory!

No doubt about it, high school is a tough time. Every child wants to be popular, but not everyone can be. As a parent, do you worry that your child is not popular enough?

Think back to Aesop's fable of the tortoise and the hare. Recall that the hare, in spite of his big talk, lost the race. The tortoise, in a quietly unassuming way beat the socks off the rabbit! This story is no fable. In the game of life, the nerd usually wins. If your child is a quiet, unassuming turtle in high school, research strongly suggests that ultimately he'll beat the popular kids at their own game. While the in-crowd talks a good game in high school, they tend to stagnate in their own past glories. As a result, the quiet kid who studied hard often surpasses the popular kid with greater and longer-lasting success.

What's the cheap psychological trick? In life's race, actions of substance always beat out empty words and popularity. The hare has his past glory, but the tortoise has the future!

REFERENCE

Lamb, D. H., and G. D. Reeder. "Reliving Golden Days." *Psychology Today* June (1986): 22–30.

Cheap Trick No. 6

Dutch Treats

T was the night before Christmas, and all through the house, not a creature was stirring—and they had all removed their shoes. Children in the Netherlands, Belgium, and Luxembourg celebrate St. Nicholas' Day by placing their shoes on the doorstep, filled with cookies and candy for the saint. St. Nicholas takes the goodies and leaves a gift for the child. Positive reinforcement theory guarantees that a similar technique will work in all sorts of situations. But the positive reinforcement must be a surprise and may only be used after your child has behaved well. Here's a simple example.

Many parents nag their children to remove their muddy shoes when they enter the house. Most use punishment when the child does not comply. A smart parent will do the opposite. On the rare occasion that your child does what you request— without your nagging—smile and say nothing. But when he's not looking, put a small surprise in his shoes. When he finds his little gift, he may continue to put his shoes at the door without prompting, hoping that he will be rewarded again.

Use the same trick when you're having trouble getting your child to take a nap. When he spontaneously takes a nap without you demanding it, place a safe surprise in his crib or bed for when he wakes up. Next time, your child may want to go to sleep because he knows there will be a reward waiting when he wakes up.

What's the cheap psychological trick? A small, surprise token of your esteem can work wonders and may assure that the behavioral change you desire will be seen again.

REFERENCE

Hall, R. V., and M. C. Hall. *How to Select Reinforcers.* Austin, TX: Pro-Ed, Inc., 1998.

Cheap Trick No. 7

Speak Up!

Parents always wish their children could talk before they are able to and wouldn't talk so much after they begin. Nevertheless, it's important that parents realize the power of words and do everything they can to maximize language skills. Here are some cheap psychological tricks you can use from the day of birth to get your child ready for speaking.

Talk to your child. No baby talk. Clear, complete simple sentences spoken in a quiet voice work best; children are naturally afraid of loud sounds. No "goo-goos," no "ga-gas," no "mommie's prewcious wuttle bwaby." No diminutive, quasi-child-like sounds. Remember, your child will imitate you as she grows older.

Teach your child how to sign. Children can't talk

until both their jaws and vocal cords are developmentally ready, but they've learned many words long before their little mouths can express them. Check out a sign language book at your local library. Learn basic words for "milk," "juice," "potty," and other age-appropriate terms. Teach your child to sign by saying a word and physically signing it at the same time. Then don't be surprised when your pre-talking toddler comes up to you and asks for an apple using sign language. Remember, children can understand words long before they have the musculature to speak them.

Have books in the house. It doesn't matter if they are Little Golden Books or leather-bound tomes. A great deal of research has shown that the mere presence of books in a home increases a child's verbal skills and enhances his love of language. Some research has shown that having books in the home helps even when the parent never reads to the child. Teach your child a love of books, and he'll carry this regard throughout his lifetime, even after he discovers computers.

Teach your child the words for colors. These words can give you a major clue about his speech abilities. Color names contain most of the sounds youngsters need to pronounce words properly. If he has trouble saying a particular color, then you'll be forewarned as to the possibility of a speech impediment. Remember, give your child time to develop—his body must catch up with his brains—so don't be too quick to rush to judgment.

Teach your child big words. While adults may think big words are too difficult, children love them and can master them surprisingly well. Just ask any child who's fascinated with dinosaurs to tell you their long, scientific names. They can do it, and do it with alacrity. Learning to pronounce and remember big words will help your child develop a love of language.

What's the cheap psychological trick? Walt Disney was right: "Education and entertainment are not enemies." Start early and make language fun, and your child will carry a love of words with her throughout her life—and your future grandchildren's lives, too!

REFERENCE

Waxman, S. P., and T. Kosowski. "Nouns Mark Category Relations: Toddlers' and Preschoolers' Word-learning Biases." *Child Development* 61 (1990): 1461–1473.

TV or Not TV?

To TV or not to TV? That is the question. (Admittedly, it's fractured Shakespeare, but the point's worth considering.) The average family watches thirty hours of television per week, 1560 hours a year. Each year, that family spends sixty-five days of their lives in front of the television, watching—among other things—17,000 commercials.

In addition to the obvious—programs may be teaching your children lessons you don't want them to learn—television may actually hinder the development of children under the age of five. This is the one time in their little lives when they can easily master the art of entertaining themselves. If they spend too much time in front of a television, they never learn how. Instead, they'll grow up expecting to be entertained rather than realizing they have the potential, the ability, and the smarts to do it themselves.

How do you know if your young child is suffering from too much television exposure? Easy. How often does she tell you she's bored? If you hear this phrase often, then your child has not mastered the art of self-entertainment. When she says there's nothing to do, respond with "What are you going to do about it?" Listen for her answer, and then redirect her thinking toward painting, drawing, writing, and other solitary activities that are self-entertaining.

It's also important to limit computer time for the same reason. Today's computers do more and more for the users. The medium entertains actively while the child responds passively. The result: She grows up expecting to be entertained without learning how to entertain herself.

You may want to ban the word "bored" from your household. Many parents have concluded that this word is just as offensive as an expletive. They have informed their children that they don't ever want them to use that word again. It may sound silly, but it teaches the child to take responsibility for his own boredom and to do something about it.

What's the cheap psychological trick? There's a brief window of opportunity during which your child can learn to entertain herself. If the television or the computer is on too much during this period, she might not learn how. Turn off the television to turn on the creativity.

REFERENCE

Huston, A. C., J. C. Wright, M. L. Rice, D. Kerkman, and M. St. Peters. "Development of Television Viewing Patterns in Early Childhood: A Longitudinal Investigation." *Developmental Psychology* 26 (1990): 409–420.

Cheap Trick No. 9

Spare the Rod?

How many spankings do you think the typical preschool child receives in a year? Would you guess one a month? One a week? The answer will surprise you. The average preschooler receives as many as 150 spankings a year. That averages out to one spanking every 2.4 days.

A lot of parents follow the maxim "Spare the rod and spoil the child." Five out of every six parents regularly spank their children. Some think spanking is an effective form of discipline. Others don't have a clue, and most use corporal punishment because it's the only way they know how to discipline their children. After all, their parents used it on them, and they're no worse for the wear, so how bad can it be? As a result, many parents use only corporal punishment and have never felt the need to learn other, even more powerful techniques.

Most people think the phrase "Spare the rod and spoil the child" is biblical. In fact, it first appeared in the poem "Hudibras" by the English satirical poet Samuel Butler. Interestingly enough, this man also wrote "Dildoides," a long poem about sexual substitutes.

When it comes to the rod and the child, there are several things you need to know:

✂ Spanking does not work on every child. To paraphrase Gilbert and Sullivan in *The Mikado,* the punishment must fit the child. If it does not, it will have little effect. Parents must know their child well enough to know what works and what does not. As a result, parents need to know and use more than one method of discipline.

✂ When parents use corporal punishment too much and in response to every offense, it loses its power. Spanking a child for every infraction actually confuses more than it disciplines.

✂ Spanking teaches aggression. Moreover, it turns the parent into the aggressor and virtually ensures that your child will spank her children. It also teaches that hitting can solve a problem. Children who are spanked (but not abusively) for behaving aggressively tend to become more aggressive.

🖋 Spanking a child inhibits *all* behaviors, not just the one you're trying to stop.

🖋 If you are truly angry with your child, don't use corporal punishment. It's a form of discipline that should only be used when the parent is calm.

🖋 Administer punishment within minutes of misbehavior. The parent who sees the behavior should deliver the punishment immediately instead of waiting until the other parent gets home to do it.

🖋 If you must spank, use an open hand rather than a closed fist. If the punishment hurts your hand, that's a signal that you've gone too far.

🖋 Corporal punishment may not stop the behavior it is intended to. It will always, however, teach the child to avoid being caught.

What's the cheap psychological trick? Should you use corporal punishment? You need to weigh this decision carefully. If you use spanking as your only method of discipline, you're not parenting. If spanking your child truly hurts you emotionally more than it hurts your child, then at least you're doing it right. Because there are so many other, far more effective techniques, corporal punishment should be used only as a last resort.

REFRENCE

Baumrind, D. "Does Causally Relevant Research Support a Blanket Injunction against Disciplinary Spanking by Parents?" Invited Address at the 109th Annual Convention of the American Psychological Association. San Francisco, California, August 24, 2001.

Zacks, R. *An Underground Education.* New York: Doubleday, 1997.

Cheap Trick No. 10

When Authority Speaks

Meet the hypothetical Mr. Sawyer. He genuinely dislikes authority figures. He wants to rebel, to fight, to stand up for himself, even when he knows he's wrong. Wonder where he learned this attitude? You might be surprised.

The likelihood is that he had a parent who not just corrected, but overcorrected him for the least infraction. When Mr. Sawyer's father corrected his son, he harped on the same issue over and over and over. And he corrected his son in public, in front of others—strangers even.

This kind of parenting will cause problems later. It's the correction compounded by embarrassment that leads to contempt for those in authority.

What's the cheap psychological trick? Remember the following quote. It's attributed to Solon, who was Archon (mayor/magistrate) of the ancient City of Athens. He reminded parents to "Reprove your child privately; commend them publicly. Make the reproof short and to the point; make the commendation long and glorious." Discipline should be a private experience between parent and child. Never correct your child in public, unless it is absolutely unavoidable. Censuring a child in front of others too often and with little thought is humiliating and unproductive.

REFERENCE

Feldman, S. S., and K. R. Wentzel. "The Relationship between Parenting Styles, Sons' Self-restraint, and Peer Relations in Early Adolescence." *Journal of Early Adolescence* 10 (1990): 439–454.

Self-esteem = Abilities ÷ Aspirations

Self-esteem is a lot like the weather. Everybody talks about it, but very few people understand exactly what causes it. According to talk shows, it's the panacea for the world's problems. Any time anyone has a problem, the first pop psychological explanation that comes to mind is low self-esteem.

There's no question that people need more self-esteem. The only problem is that they don't know what it is, how to get it, and perhaps most important of all, how to keep it.

William James, the first American psychologist, defined self-esteem way back in 1890. In fact, he provided the following formula:

$$\text{Self-esteem} = \text{Abilities} \div \text{Aspirations}$$

Self-esteem, sometimes referred to as self-confidence, equals your abilities—what you can do—divided by your aspirations—what you want to do. The better you are at things you want to do, the greater your self esteem. Do you want your child to have greater self-esteem? Figure out ways that she can learn how to do things—and do them well—for herself. Here are some ways to help her.

First, don't be so quick to do things for your child. Give her the opportunity to learn by doing. Follow the model used to teach medical students: (1) See one; (2) do one; then (3) teach one. Let your child watch you; then let her try it on her own. Finally, let her show you how herself.

Next, beware of extracurricular overkill, which can make your child a generalist in everything and an expert in nothing. Instead concentrate on two or three activities that your child can master. Her self-esteem will be linked to the things she can do well, not the number of things she can do.

Finally, listen to your child. When she stops talking about some behavior she once enjoyed, something's up. Either she's grown tired of it, or she's realized she'll never master it. When a child stops talking about something they once enjoyed, forcing her to continue does more harm than good.

What's the cheap psychological trick? Helping your child match her abilities with her aspirations is smart parenting and one of the best ways to ensure self-esteem.

REFERENCES

James, W. *Psychology: The Briefer Course.* New York: Henry Holt & Company, 1920.

James, W. *The Principles of Psychology.* New York: Dover Publishing, 1950.

PART II

THE DETAILS

"You know more than you think you do."

—BENJAMIN SPOCK

Cheap Trick No. 12

Easy Does It!

Believe it or not, kids will do just about anything you ask, providing you get down on their level and explain it. Children want your love, your praise, and your attention. When your children misbehave, do you jump to conclusions and feel convinced that they are becoming rebellious? Remember: What you think is rebellion may actually be your child's inability to perform the assigned task. Find an easy way for your child to do what you need him to do, and both of you will be happier.

Want your child to hang up his coat when he comes in from school? Sounds like a reasonable request, especially if you're an adult. Then why does your child throw his coat on the chair or table instead? Is he being rebellious? Maybe, but not likely. Ask yourself some questions about the situation. For example, is my child tall enough to reach the coat hook? If not, he's trying to do what you ask, but he can't. Try lowering the hooks. If you make the task easy to perform, the child will probably do as you ask.

Want your child to zip up his coat on a wintry cold day? First, take a look at the coat. Chances are the zipper looks just like yours. Some zippers are not designed for children's hands; small fingers may have difficulty manipulating them. If you want to make it easier for your young one to zip his coat, attach a key ring to the end of the zipper. Small hands will find the ring easier to grasp.

What's the cheap psychological trick? If you make it easy for a child to perform a task, he's more likely to comply. Make sure you praise him when he does.

REFERENCE

Lamb, M. E. "What Can Research Experts Tell Parents about Effective Socialization? In E. F. Zigler, M. E. Lamb, and I. L. Child (Eds.), *Socialization and Personality Development.* New York: Oxford University Press, 1982.

Cheap Trick No. 13

The Nine-Foot Rule

Think about the last time you visited a major theme park. You probably noticed how clean it was. You might assume that a large crew of street sweepers keeps the park so tidy (and you might wish that they could help you out at home as well). But that's not the case. With thousands of people visiting the parks each day, an army couldn't keep it clean without the assistance of the guests. How does park management ensure that assistance? It's easy. They follow the nine-foot rule, and you can use it at home as well.

When a park guest consumes her soda, she'll look around for a trash receptacle. If she sees one within nine feet, then it's likely that she'll walk over to it and discard her rubbish there. If it's more than ten feet away, she'll be forced to make a conscious decision—*Should I walk over there or throw it on the ground?* If the distance is more than nine feet, it's likely that she'll leave her empty container precisely where she finished it.

If you want the members of your family to pick up after themselves, then make sure there's a trash receptacle within their immediate field of vision. Don't hide it. Buy an attractive trash can and place it squarely within your family's path.

If you want your child to pick up his dirty clothes, put the hamper within nine feet of his favorite strip-down spot. Remember the old adage, "Out of sight, out of mind." If the hamper is unseen and the floor is available, then the floor becomes the depository of choice. If you want your child to be more studious, prioritize, print, and place your most important rules of behavior (no more than three rules, please) within nine feet of your child's desk or work surface. This visual cue will remind your children of your expectations.

What's the cheap psychological trick? If you want your child to pay attention, make sure that the important tools are well within his sight.

REFERENCE

Kohn, A. "You Know What They Say." *Psychology Today* 22 (April, 1988): 36–41.

Cheap Trick No. 14

Curses Foiled Again

There are thousands and thousands of words in the English language, all designed to help you get your point across. Some of them are simple, many expressive, quite a few creative, some downright funny, and a small number crude. Unfortunately, many people rely too heavily on a very small number of vulgarities to express themselves; this can be a particular problem for teenagers. Here's a cheap psychological trick that will help stop profanity right in its track.

Does your child have a knack for finding the right vulgarity at the wrong time? If she's too old for time-out and you have failed to make your point with fining and grounding, try a Cursing Jar.

Start with a jar full of quarters. Put an amount of money in the jar that's equivalent to something your child wants to purchase— say $50 worth of quarters or the equivalent of a new video game.

Explain to your child that the contents of this jar will belong to her at the end of four weeks if she can refrain from swearing. (It takes at least that long to stop a nasty habit.) Mark that date on the calendar. Place the jar in a prominent place in the house. It's important to use a transparent container so the child can see what she's working for.

Each time your child uses a curse word or slang expression—one that you've told her is inappropriate— remove a predetermined amount of money (less with younger children and more with older). Each time, remove the same amount of money without reprobation. Make sure you do this while the child watches. The removal is not subject to debate; it's just removed upon each infraction. At the end of the designated period, give all the remaining money in the jar to your child and remind her of how much money was lost due to her choice of language. Give the money lost to a charity of your child's choice.

What's the cheap psychological trick? If you believe this cheap psychological trick is tantamount to buying your child's good behavior, you're correct. But it may work when other discipline methods fail. Bottom line: Curses foiled again.

REFERENCE

Bodnar, J. *Dollars & Sense for Kids.* Washington, D.C.: Kiplinger Books, 1999.

Made of Money

Kids and adults think of money in radically different ways. Kids believe adults are made of money, and adults know their children don't appreciate how hard they have to work for money. You can use a cheap psychological trick to teach your kids to look at money from an adult point of view. But it's a bit of tough love, and not all experts agree it's the best way.

You could require your child to earn his allowance by completing assigned household chores. According to a recent study, 88 percent of all parents believe this is the best strategy. The remaining 12 percent disagree; they think family responsibilities shouldn't have a price, but they don't offer an alternate technique that teaches a responsible work ethic. Until they do, here's a two-prong cheap psychological strategy that is endorsed by 88 percent of the population.

As a general rule, a child's weekly allowance should be equal to one dollar for each year of his age, so a ten-year-old child would receive ten dollars a week. Of course, this figure must be adjusted to fit the financial means of the family.

Payment of that allowance should be tied to successful completion of chores: If you don't take out the trash, then you forfeit your allowance. This approach teaches the American ethic of earning money the old-fashioned way—through hard work. Instead of referring to your child's responsibilities as "chores," start early in his life and call them his family job.

What's the cheap psychological trick? A penny earned is a penny valued, and more likely a penny saved. Imagine how valuable this ethic will be as your little child grows up and enters the workforce.

REFERENCE
"Money" *Parenting* (November, 1995): 149.

Dear Santa

You can learn a lot from a child's letters to Santa. Even though the holidays are now a very commercial time of the year and most kids seem to want everything they see, you should be looking for the "Christmas Constant."

Over the years, the number of gifts on a typical child's "wish list" has remained constant while the number of presents parents buy for them has increased. The average child asks for three to four presents, but the average parent now gives her child between seven and eight presents.

On the surface, this may look generous and loving, but there's more going on under the wrapping. It's a very subtle issue that can cause problems later on. Giving

more than has been requested tends to diminish the initial request in the recipient's eyes. It can reduce the value of your child's gifts and lead him to expect that he will always receive more than he asks for. And there's an even bigger potential problem. Overgiving reduces a child's love of the holiday and regard for the giver. In other words, give more than you should and two things happen. First, the gifts are devalued; then the giver will be devalued, too.

Why were the Wise Men so wise? They only brought three gifts. They apparently knew the psychological truth: Less is more.

What's the cheap psychological trick?
Refrain from giving your child too much, too freely, for no reason, with no strings attached. Overgiving creates conflicting expectations at all ages.

REFERENCE

Garber, S. W., M. D. Garber, and R. F. Spizman. *Good Behavior.* New York: Villard Books, 1987.

Cheap Trick No. 17

Making a List and Checking It Twice

If your child is like most other children, she starts "advising" you of her wish list immediately after the Halloween decorations are put away. After all, your kid started shopping long before Halloween. Advertisers have been targeting her wish list for months; they want to make sure their product is in your child's stocking. So, parents must answer two important questions: What gifts does my child really want? Which requests are the result of first-class, high-powered marketing strategies? Here's a cheap psychological trick that answers this question and weeds out the real Christmas or Hanukkah wishes from the holiday hype.

Early in the season, ask your child to make a list of what gifts she wants this holiday. Give her free reign;

just give her a piece of paper and a pencil to write them down or let her dictate the list to you. Keep this list.

A few weeks later, sit your child down, and ask her to make out a brand new list. Don't mention or let her look at her first list.

Now compare the two lists. What appears on both lists is what she really wants. The rest probably came from advertised hype that got her attention but didn't reach her heart.

What's the cheap psychological trick? Advertisers trade on the hype of the moment. Let some time go by between your child's lists, and the impulses and fads will have faded.

REFERENCE

Bodnar, J. *Dollars & Sense for Kids.* Washington, D.C.: Kiplinger Books, 1999.

Lost and Found

Most children have a security blanket or similar item. If you've ever left it at home—or worse, lost it—you know that they don't respond well in this situation. They just express their suffering—loudly.

Holding on to a security object—or "transitional object," in psychological parlance—is a common behavior. Approximately 90 percent of girls and 70 percent of boys have at least one special teddy bear, Raggedy Ann or Andy, or blankie that must be within sight at all times. Even in adulthood, according to one study, approximately 20 percent of women and 5 percent of men sleep with a teddy bear.

There's a cheap psychological trick that can help if you find yourself traveling with a child and without his security object: Borrow one. You're probably not the only person who has lost something similar. While a substitute may not be identical to the original, it can be a substantial time-saver and mood-soother.

Imagine you're settling in for a good night's sleep in a hotel room and your child suddenly realizes his "wobbie" is missing. Before you spend bucks on some piece of new rodent plush at the gift shop, go to the front desk, explain your situation, and see if they have a collection of lost security objects that have been misplaced by other hotel guests. Borrow—they might just give it to you—a similar looking teddy, tell your child that this new one is teddy's brother or sister, and that old teddy is home waiting. You may just buy yourself enough time to get through the evening and get home.

Finally, to keep from losing something important— from security blanket to teddy bear to important papers for the teacher—remember the cheap trick that's a bane for the gods of lost objects. Safety pins. Remember how mom pinned those important notes to your person in the first grade? It still works. Even the most active or forgetful child can't lose an important object that's been pinned to her clothing.

What's the cheap psychological trick? Enlist
your child in helping to track personal items
before they're lost. But in a pinch, finders keepers, especially if you know where to look.

REFERENCE

Shafii, T. "The Prevalence and Use of Transitional Objects: A Study of 230
Adolescents." *Journal of American Academy of Child Psychiatry* 25
(November, 1986): 805–808.

Makes Scents

Here's a way to stay in your child's mind even when you're out of his sight. Whether you'll just be away overnight or for a longer period, this trick works and works well. Take your usual cologne or perfume and spray it on your child's favorite stuffed animal or doll—preferably the one he sleeps with. Just like Pavlov's dogs, your child will make the association: You and his favorite toy. While you may not be present in the home, you're present in his mind.

Smell is a powerful and unique sense. Information taken in by the other four senses—sight, hearing, touch, and taste—goes to the hypothalamus, a relay station in the brain. It is then individually routed to the specific part of the brain where that sense is interpreted. Smell, on the other hand, goes straight to its interpretation point in the brain with no pause for relay. Researchers believe that our sense of smell works in this manner as a result of a prehistoric necessity. Back then, it was essential to smell a predator long before you could see it. As a result, smells move quickly through the brain, retaining powerful associations that can be attached to specific persons, places, and things.

What's the cheap psychological trick? Smell is a powerful sense, and one that connects directly with emotions. If you can't be with your child, make sure that your scent is there to remind him of your love. Makes scents.

REFERENCE

Pavlov, I. P. *Conditioned Reflexes: An Investigation of the Physiological Activity of the Cerebral Cortex.* London: Oxford University Press, 1927.

Cheap Trick No. 20

Stick With Me, Kid

Traveling is stressful in the best of circumstances and even more so these days, with safety concerns, long lines at security, and lost luggage. But imagine how high your stress would be if you lost one of your most valuable possessions—or even your child. There are travel precautions you can take that will protect both you and your children.

Once upon a time it was over the river and through the woods (snow optional) to grandma's house. Today it's rush to the airport, take two hours to clear security, hurry to board your plane, scramble to gather your belongings before you board, fly fast, and then scurry to get your checked luggage before thieves get to it. To combat this problem, do *not* use a fashionable new suitcase when you travel.

Thieves tend to avoid unique, easily recognizable pieces of luggage in favor of new, generic looking suitcases. If you do have new luggage, buy some outlandish bumper stickers—something no respectable thief would be caught carrying—and place them squarely on your suitcase. It may sound silly, but this will make your luggage unique, and thus help to keep predators at bay.

Do the same thing for your children, but don't—no matter how much you'd like to—check them as luggage. The French moralist, La Rochefoucauld, said, "Those incapable of committing great crimes do not readily suspect them of others." Translated: You would never think about taking another person's child, but child snatchers are alive and well at airports, amusement parks, sports arenas, and other places where children are

present. To keep this traumatic event from happening to your family, mark your child in a distinctive place—his shoes.

When a child is lost, authorities first ask, "What kind of shoes were they wearing?" People who abduct young children may take them into a restroom, dye their hair, discard their clothing, and provide a new unidentifiable outfit for them to wear. Rarely do they change a child's shoes. Make sure that your child can be readily identified by his shoes—by brand, color, laces, stickers, printed words—but never the child's name or initials.

What's the cheap psychological trick? Identifiable marks are your best protection for all your possessions, especially your most valuable ones. And don't forget to hold small children firmly by the hand!

REFERENCE

De Becker, G. *Protecting the Gift: Keeping Children and Teenagers Safe (And Parents Sane)*. New York: Dell Books, 2000.

Cheap Trick No. 21

Do You Know Where Your Children Are?

O nce upon a time, many local television stations started their late-evening broadcasts with "It's eleven o'clock. Do you know where your children are?" Perhaps that phrase reflected a genuine concern, or maybe it was merely designed to catch the public's attention and increase the station's ratings. But whatever the motivation, that familiar TV announcement contained a clue to a cheap but valuable psychological trick that is just plain smart today.

Parents should be particularly vigilant at two particular periods in the day: From noon until six PM and from eleven PM until four AM. Here's why.

The afternoon is a dangerous time. Parents are often at work, and children have time on their hands after school. Statistics show that most child abductions occur between lunchtime and dinnertime, and children are most likely to try illegal drugs between four and six PM.

The wee hours of the morning are the original devil's hours. During the Middle Ages, many people believed that the devil was most likely to take their souls at three o'clock in the morning—an hour that was associated with the Holy Trinity. They were right to worry about this time of day. According to the circadian or body clock timing system, the body is most fatigued—and thus most accident prone—between eleven PM and four AM.

What's the cheap psychological trick? Keep an eye on the clock and pay attention to where your children are during their most vulnerable times of the day. When the television news broadcast began with "It's eleven o'clock. Do you know where you children are?" they were giving parents a valuable reminder.

REFERENCES

Grilly, D. M. *Drugs and Human Behavior.* Boston: Allyn & Bacon, 1992.

Cheap Trick No. 22

Fire!

When daylight savings time rolls around, most people are conditioned to check the batteries in their smoke detectors. Smart. Very smart. But did you remember to go over the family fire drill routine? It takes less than five minutes and could save your children's lives.

Each year more than one thousand youngsters age nine and under die in fires in the home. So teach your kids how to perform a fire drill as soon as they are able to follow directions. Here are the steps:

Step 1: Create a family evacuation plan. Work this out with all family members so they know what they're supposed to do.

Step 2: Walk through the evacuation plan. Just rehearse it. Make a game out of it, but keep it serious enough that the children learn exactly what's expected of them should a real fire occur.

Step 3: Question your children. When you're driving to school, soccer practice, or dance class, ask your child, "What are the steps in our fire drill? What are you supposed to do? Where are you supposed to go? Where are we supposed to meet if we're separated?"

Step 4: Call a fire drill. Actually, you should practice two different types of fire drills. First, an announced one. Let all family members know that there will be a fire drill and tell them when it will occur. No surprise. Later on, call a surprise fire drill—with smoke detectors blaring and everything.

Step 5: Right those wrongs. Go over all that happened. Correct, praise, and caution where appropriate. This debriefing is the time to make sure your family has what it takes to come out of a fire alive.

What's the cheap psychological trick? An ounce of fire prevention is worth a pound of cure. Make a habit of family fire drills when your kids are small. Even if you agree that it's a good thing to do, the research says you're the exception—unfortunately—to the rule if you actually follow through with a real family fire drill.

REFERENCE
Uncommon sense

PART III

THE BODY

"Health… is the first and greatest of all blessings."

—Lord Chesterfield

Jumping to Conclusions

Would you rather your child have an emotional or a physical problem? If you're like most parents, your first answer would probably be "neither." But when forced to choose, many parents will pick physical problems over emotional. Why? A physical problem is usually easy to understand, is often easier to treat, and carries little or no stigma. Yet when children perform poorly in school, a high percentage of adults are quick to suggest an emotional problem as the cause.

Start with a child who's not performing in school. Some people will blame the child first, believing that he's either not capable of the work or not living up to his potential. The more "sophisticated" folks might blame the problem on a learning disability or an emotional crisis.

A small group of people, usually older adults, might instead attribute such a problem to a physical cause such as a hearing or vision problem. It can't be that easy, right? Frankly, it *can* be that easy.

According to what social psychologists refer to as a "fundamental attribution error" and/or "correspondence bias," humans are programmed to blame another's inadequacies on their personality traits or emotional disposition. Rarely do we consider a physical difficulty as the cause of failure or poor performance. It's just the way we think these days. Smart parents should always check for physical limitations and get them addressed first.

What's the cheap psychological trick? Make sure your child is checked for obvious infirmities like visual and hearing problems before he's given a barrage of fancy diagnostic tests.

REFERENCE

Gilbert, D. T., and P. S. Malone. "The Correspondence Bias." *Psychological Bulletin* 117 (1995): 21–38.

Cheap Trick No. 24

Left Is All Right

Just because "left" isn't "right" doesn't make it wrong. Yet, there's a stigma associated with the word "left"—left-handed compliments, left behind, leftover, left out, out in left field. Fortunately this stigma isn't anywhere near the problem it was a couple of decades ago. Today, as a group, lefties are really all right, but they still have a lot to deal with in today's society.

Left-handed people are governed by both written and unwritten bills of "rights." Even our language works against them. For instance, there's no fair shake in an allegedly neutral word like "ambidextrous," which translates literally to "right-handed on both sides." The Greek word for "left-handed," *aristera,* may remind us of the word aristocrat, which means "those fit to govern." A group of outstanding lefties includes Tiberius, Alexander the Great, and Queen Victoria, as well as Harry S. Truman, James Garfield, and George W. Bush.

The advent of tools and the uniformity of their design indirectly have created a preference for the right. There are more right-handed people, so most equipment is designed for their use.

Studies suggest that left-handed children are clumsier and more accident-prone than those who are right-handed. Of course, if the shoe was on the other foot and all of the equipment was designed for lefties, the right-handed people might be clumsy, too.

Don't overprotect your lefty. She's going to have to learn to live in a right-handed world. Nevertheless, help her out when you can. If you're the parent of a left-handed child, you should be aware of the potential for more accidents and you should protect your child accordingly.

❋ Store snacks in an overhead cabinet which opens to the right.

❋ Put your little lefty at the left corner of the table and avoid dueling elbows during mealtimes

❋ Make sure she wears a bike helmet.

❋ Provide writing instruments that don't smear, and scissors, notebooks, and other school supplies that are lefty friendly.

❋ Monitor the use of tools (especially potentially dangerous ones) that are right-handed until she gets the hang of them.

What's the cheap psychological trick? Keep an eye out for your lefty and make sure she doesn't get hurt out in the world of right-handed folks.

REFERENCE

Allman, W. F. "Do Lefties or Righties Have the Upper Hand?" *Hippocrates,* (September/October, 1987): 98.

Cheap Trick No. 25

First Aid Firsts

The only thing worse than hurting yourself is see-ing your child injured. Fortunately, science—and Mom and Dad—has provided us with a few useful maneuvers to distract our loved ones from their pain and speed their healing process. So when your child comes to you with his latest boo-boo, try the following tactics.

Start with a "Shhhh." Parents, as well as social sci-entists, know that infants and toddlers (even adults under the influence of alcohol) prefer and respond to soft soothing sounds like whispers and "shhhhs." Loud noises tend to arouse or startle, but subtle whispered speech can mitigate pain, divert fear, and provide com-fort. (Additionally, whispering or reducing the volume of your voice has been shown to be an effective means of reducing both the emotional impact and the duration of an argument.)

Rub the injured area, kiss it, and hide the sharp medical instruments. This approach combines the power of touch with a little sensory diversion.

If your child has a splinter embedded in his little finger, he's probably dreading the needle he thinks you'll use to remove it. Surprise him. Try scotch tape first. Apply the tape over the splinter; it may adhere to the painful object and extract it. This trick also buys time, allowing the child to calm down. If it works, the child will think you're a genius. If not, and a needle is necessary—or medical assistance, for that matter—remember the old executioner's trick. Allow the victim to turn his head before you unveil the axe.

Every child will fall down, hurt himself, and spill a drop of blood or two. And every parent knows that the smallest amount of blood can precipitate gobs of sobs. If you use a light-colored cloth to mop up the blood, the results look much worse; each blotting reveals previous and current blood stains right before your child's eyes. Here's a trick that makes the blood and some of the pain go away. Next time your child comes running and screaming, with blood streaming, use a clean, red cloth to soak up the blood. It will camouflage the bloodstains.

Of course, it goes without saying: Follow first aid procedures and see a physician if necessary.

What's the cheap psychological trick? Psychologists would say this trick comes from the research on "object permanence"—if your child doesn't see evidence of his pain, he won't feel it as strongly. Mom and Dad would say it's just common sense. They're both right.

REEFERENCE

Piaget, J. *The Child's Conception of the World.* New York: Harcourt & Brace, 1929.

Healing Hospital Fears

There's one thing kids of all ages will admit: Hospitals are scary places. It doesn't matter if you're three, thirty, or ninety-three, hospitals are just no fun. There are the antiseptic smells and the needle sticks, the poking and the prodding, and don't forget the pain and the promises that it will all be over soon. So, if you need to take your child to the hospital, here are some guidelines:

(1) Be honest. Make sure that you give your child an honest explanation for his visit to the hospital, especially if an operation is involved. Also, if possible—and certainly seek medical guidance here—postpone elective surgeries until at least age three, when a child is better able to understand what you tell her.

(2) Avoid surprises. Go to your friendly local librarian and ask him for a book about a child who's going to have surgery. The librarian can easily identify any number of books. Reading your child stories about hospitals may remove the surprises and address their fears.

(3) Explain the difference between anesthesia and regular sleep. It's important for your child to know that this is a special kind of sleep during which he'll feel no pain. Make sure you explain that this sleep is temporary and he'll wake up with you nearby.

(4) Show lots of affection. No doubt you love your child, and no doubt you show that love regularly. During surgery and hospital time, make sure you lavish him with extra attention and affection. You may think this is for the child—and it will do wonders for him—but it will also help to quell your fears. Also, don't forget your spouse, who'll need attention, too. When a hospital's involved, you just can't have too much affection.

(5) Allow the anger. Don't be surprised if your child decides to pitch a tantrum. This is one time that it's okay. After all, what the doctor's doing is rather invasive, and adults don't like it either.

(6) Stay with your child as long as you can. If your child has established a great rapport with the doctor, ask the physician if he or she will walk your child—hand-in-hand—to the operating room. If the doctor agrees, put her on your holiday card list and the speed dial, and definitely write a thank-you note. If this plan isn't feasible, ask your doctor if the anesthetic can be started while the child is still in his own hospital room before he goes to the operating room. This will reduce the child's fear of being alone during a vulnerable time. Going to sleep in familiar surroundings, with family and toys around, reduces fears, and you—the parent—get to spend more time comforting your child.

What's the cheap psychological trick? Prepare your child for the experience and look to your doctor to help you ease your child's fears during a stressful time. Hospitals are no fun. The pain can't be totally removed, but love does wonders reducing fears and discomfort.

REFERENCE

Bakwin, H., and R. M. Bakwin. *Behavior Disorders in Children.* Philadelphia: W. B. Saunders Company, 1972.

Rock and Roll

There's a form of rock and roll that's quite good for you and your child, but it has nothing to do with music, and it won't affect your hearing. Parents have always sworn by the power of the rocking chair. Why does it work so well? Rocking, or any form of gentle swaying, stimulates the vestibular system of the body, which sends information to the brain, telling it how your head is moving through space. Many people aren't even aware of their vestibular systems. But if you've ever suffered from a balance problem, you have first-hand knowledge of its importance. Rocking is soothing and enjoyable because it gently stimulates this vital system and improves circulation, especially to the extremities.

Every parent knows that rocking a child to sleep is

soothing to the child, and to the parent, too! But did you know that babies who are rocked regularly gain weight faster? Not only does rocking stimulate the vestibular system, but it also provides an opportunity for touch and intimacy with another human.

What's the cheap psychological trick? This is one form of rock 'n' roll that won't disturb your sleep. Rock your child to relax you both.

REFERENCES

Diamond, J., and Z. Schulz. *Exercises for Airplanes & Other Confined Spaces.* New York: Excalibur Publishing, 1996.

Cheap Trick No. 28

Teen Timing

You may think your teenager is trying to show you who's boss, but it may be his physiological sleep patterns that are exerting control. Sleep cycles change during adolescence, and your child has very little power to regulate them.

The body's circadian system is a twenty-four- to twenty-six-hour (if allowed to freely run) body clock that controls the bodily functions throughout the entire day. Sleep is one of those functions.

Kids going through puberty experience a body clock shift; their circadian system moves forward about two to three hours. The first thing you'll notice is that your teen is staying up later and sleeping later.

You and your prepubescent children may have no

trouble getting up and out at seven o'clock in the morning if you've had ample sleep. If, however, you were required to get up at four o'clock in the morning—a departure from your routine—you'd find yourself moving slowly. That's what's going on in your teenager's body. It may be seven o'clock to you, but the typical teenager's body is responding as if it's four AM. Adolescents experiencing pubertal changes are suffering from perpetual jet lag.

More and more school systems are acquiescing to the power of this circadian clock by starting classes for teenagers at nine o'clock in the morning instead of at the usual 7:30 to 8:00 AM. If your school system does not accommodate these legitimate, uncontrollable physiological changes, make sure your teenager schedules his least difficult classes—those he can literally do in his sleep—early in the morning when his body clock is still asleep. Schedule those courses that are exceedingly difficult or that will be essential for his desired profession after nine AM. His body will be up and running more efficiently by then.

Finally, don't worry if your teenage child stays up late. He's not being stubborn and rebellious; he's just not sleeping because his body clock hasn't signaled that it's time to go to bed yet.

What's the cheap psychological trick? No matter how much you complain, your child's body clock doesn't listen. Your teen may try to do as you ask, but physiology will win out. If your school system does not make allowances for this situation, you'll have to help your child plan his schedule to beat the clock.

REFERENCE

Moore-Ede, M. C., F. M. Sulzman, and C. A. Fuller. *The Clocks That Time Us.* Cambridge, MA: Harvard University Press, 1982.

Keeping the Nighttime Dry

If your child wets the bed—and every child will at some point—don't make a big deal out of it. Your child is more embarrassed about it than you are. First of all, a medical examination is in order. Common causes of bedwetting include stress, a small bladder capacity, and occasionally a urinary tract infection. Once you've ruled out any medical explanation, use this trick to put her mind at ease.

Buy pastel yellow sheets. Don't laugh, just do it. The first step toward resolving bedwetting is to remove the stigma. If your child is required to sleep on plastic sheets, then she'll continually be reminded of her problem, which won't help her get past it. Put a yellow sheet on top of the plastic sheet, and the next morning, even if she's wet the bed, the stigma will be minimized.

If you think that laziness is a cause for bedwetting, think again. Your child doesn't like it any better than you do. So bear in mind, punishment is not a solution.

You can try bed alarms, which sound in response to a few drops of urine; the gentle alarm reminds your child that her bladder is full. There are also medications, but they only help temporarily. However, they can provide a world of temporary relief for her while she's at camp or is spending nights away from home.

Finally, remember most children grow out of bed-wetting, and they usually follow a family pattern. Oftentimes, boys stop wetting the bed at the same age their fathers did; girls at the same age as their mothers.

What's the cheap psychological trick? Get chronic bedwetting checked out medically. Once you've ruled out a medical cause, use yellow sheets or a bed alarm rather than punishment to address the situation. And remember that your child will likely outgrow this problem.

REFERENCE

Bakwin, H., and R. M. Bakwin. *Behavior Disorders in Children.* Philadelphia: W. B. Saunders Company, 1972: 432–446.

Cheap Trick No. 30

Aiming to Please

How do you potty train little boys? It's a dilemma that has caused many parents to wonder momentarily why they had children in the first place.

The day of cloth diapers is over. Today's diapers are far more absorbent—fewer spills, leaks, messes, and smells. As a result, children are being potty trained about a year later than their predecessors of previous generations. Why? A dirty diaper is much less uncomfortable than it used to be; the discomfort of a dirty cloth diaper encouraged a child to try the potty. Today's children are in no hurry, and parents often have more pressing issues. Nevertheless, potty training—like death and taxes—is inevitable.

Little girls are usually easier to potty train than little boys because there's less aiming involved. Boys need cheap psychological tricks, and as sure as both big and little boys like to write their name in the snow, these approaches work! At least you can make it fun for your son.

Boys like to make noise. Put a small pie pan in the toilet. Get dad to demonstrate what happens when the urine splatters on the pan. Your child will enjoy the sound and will probably follow dad's lead.

If the appeal of the noise wears off before potty training is completed, put a small boat or other floating object in the toilet. Using the toilet becomes a game; the object is to move the boat around without using his hands. Once again, get dad to teach this technique. Hold off teaching your son to flush after each sailing experience, or you'll need regular visits from a plumber.

Once you've got basic potty training under control, it's time for mastery. No one likes a wet toilet seat, so teach your son not to miss his mark. Use a trick that corporate America and sports stadiums find effective. Paint a target or stick a red dot in the toilet where the urine flow should be directed. It's actually possible to buy targets for the toilet at supply stores.

What's the cheap psychological trick? The challenge in toilet training little boys is getting them to aim straight. Make this challenge fun for your son and you may be more successful. Keep in mind: Every gun must have a sight. No need to explain. It's just a man thing.

REFERENCE

Lovibond, S. H. "The Mechanism of Conditioning Treatment of Enuresis." *Behaviour Research and Therapy* 1 (1963): 17–21.

Cheap Trick No. 31

Clean Bill of Health

Stick your head outside your door, and the world is a cacophony of throat clearing, hacking, and coughing. Throw in sneezing, nose-blowing, and discarding tissues, and the world's awash in germs. You may think you're safe, but if you've touched an elevator button, handled one of those chained-to-the-desk bank pens, grasped an armrest on a waiting room chair, picked up the receiver of a public phone, or used a bathroom stall—especially the middle one, the most popular—in a public rest room, you have met the enemy, and the enemy—flu germs—has met you.

It's tough to avoid germs. All it takes is one sneeze, technically referred to as a sternutation, to fill a room with malevolent microorganisms. The pressure from that violent expiration of air from the nose and mouth creates a highly atomized discharge whose spray droplets are 0.1 to 0.2 millimeters in size. At a sneeze-speed of 103.6 miles per hour, these little droplets find themselves as far as five feet from the sore throat that expelled them. These germs are now your new best friends.

Fortunately, some people out there are able to reduce their chances of being contaminated by these nasty naso-oral droplets. You can teach your child to follow their example, starting with one important rule: Wash your hands—often! It's not necessary for your child to develop a hand-washing compulsion, but it is necessary for her to know how to do it the right way.

Many people walk up to the sink, turn on the water, stick three fingers from each hand under the flow, dry them off, and walk away thinking their hands are clean. Not exactly! While most parents tell their children to wash their hands, very few show them the proper way.

Teach your child to use ample hot water and lather up with good old-fashioned soap. She should wash each finger separately for at least one or two seconds and gently scrape the palm of each hand with the fingernails of the opposite hand. While washing vigorously, she should sing two rounds of "Happy Birthday to You"; it takes that long to consign millions of germs to their death. If she has a choice, she should use the hot-air drier instead of paper towels. Also you should make sure to clip her fingernails regularly. Why give germs any extra space to grow?

When you take your child to the pediatrician, be aware that etiquette has changed. It's now perfectly acceptable to ask a physician, nurse, or other medical professional, "Have you washed your hands?" Good ones will not take offense and should respond appropriately.

What's the cheap psychological trick? Wash your hands often, wash them correctly, and teach your children to do the same.

REFERENCE

Garber, S. W., M. D. Garber, and R. F. Spizman. *Good Behavior.* New York: Villard Books, 1987.

Smells Like Teen Spirit

B abies smell wonderful. Adolescents stink. There is no way to state it delicately. Any parent who lives in the same house as a teenager's athletic shoes knows firsthand that there's no fragrance in the world that will cover up the pungent aroma of an adolescent. There's no mistaking this odor, and it's a signal that major changes are on the way.

You'll know when puberty begins to rear its ugly head. In both genders, as the skin grows coarser, pores enlarge. Sebaceous glands—fatty glands in the skin—grow active and produce oily secretions. When this happens, your teen will begin to deal with the scourge of acne, but it doesn't stop there. Along with oily secretions, armpit sweat glands begin to function even before axillary hair appears. Much to the adolescent's chagrin, the result is not just perspiration, but "teenage stink."

When these smells start to emerge, you know there's no turning back. Your child is starting to encounter the perils of puberty. You're in for a first-class physical and emotional roller coaster ride.

What's the cheap psychological trick? God has a sense of humor. He's provided us with a warning signal for the approach of adolescence. Take a deep whiff to see if you should start worrying about the perils of adolescence. There's a reason Nirvana recorded "Smells Like Teen Spirit."

REFERENCE

Tanner, J. M. "Growth Spurt, Adolescent." In R. M. Lerner, A. C. Petersen, and J. Brooks-Gunn (Eds.), *Encyclopedia of Adolescence.* New York: Garland, 1991.

Cheap Trick No. 33

Eat Your Veggies

You think your child is the only kid in the world who won't eat his veggies? Wrong! Most parents struggle with this. They cajole. They beg. They bribe. Here are some more effective ways to entice kids to eat healthy foods:

(1) Involve the child in the food selection. Get him talking about what he likes and during the conversation, implant parental wisdom about how good vegetables are for you.

(2) Involve the child in the food preparation. Give him an understanding of food, selection, meal planning, and cleanup.

(3) Avoid between-meal snacks. Since many of

today's children are overweight, cutting back on snacks is a good idea.

(4) Start him out with small portions. Kids see everything through kid-sized eyes. An adult portion of carrots looks huge to them. Once your child has eaten a small por- tion of veg- etables, then praise, praise, praise.

Now, if these approaches don't work, here's a cheap psychological trick to the rescue. Vegetables out of sight are vegetables out of mind. In other words, hide the vegetables. Hide very finely chopped vegetables in kid-friendly foods like macaroni and cheese and lasagna. Hide finely grated carrots or minced broccoli in pancakes or soup. And don't forget other baked goods. Kids who snub vegetables will often beg for carrot muffins.

What's the cheap psychological trick? Don't overwhelm your child with your demands to eat vegetables. Involve him in the food process, give him small portions, and when all else fails—hide 'em. And don't be so upset if your child really hates broccoli. After all, he could grow up to be President. It worked out all right for George H. W. Bush.

REFERENCE

Buss, D. M. *Evolutionary Psychology: The New Science of the Mind.* Needham Heights, MA: Allyn & Bacon, 1999.

Cheap Trick No. 34

Just Say No

This short trick should be easy to do, yet most parents find it exceedingly difficult to implement. Frankly, though, it doesn't make sense to ignore it. In these difficult times more and more people may entice your child to try any number of illegal chemicals. One would think that parents would be vigilant, but many are not.

Maybe parents don't follow through because they believe their children would never do such a thing; perhaps they think it's not necessary because their children have been taught repeatedly by society to "just say no." The cold hard truth is that any child, anywhere, no matter what he's been taught, is a ripe target for savvy drug salesmen. Here are some alarming facts:

❊ According to one study, 25 percent of all nine to twelve year olds have been offered illegal drugs. That's one out of every four kids. This is a conservative observational statistic.

❊ Only 7 percent of parents believed that their children in this age group were being exposed to illegal drugs. You do the math.

❊ Only 25 percent of parents reported that they had ever talked to their children about drugs. This is probably a conservative figure; more realistically, one in ten parents speak to their children on a regular basis about the perils of drug abuse.

What's the cheap psychological trick? Tell your children about the dangers of drugs. Tell them as often as you think of it. Teach them to do more than "just say no." Teach them to run away from people who offer them drugs, and teach them to report it immediately to you or an authority figure. This is one time when "tattling" is okay, appropriate, perfectly acceptable, and could save their life. Better yet, put a post-it note on your refrigerator to remind you to say, "I love you. Don't do drugs" to your children each and every day.

REFERENCE

Ladd, G. W., and K. D. LeSieur. "Parents and Peer Relationships." In M. H. Bornstein (Ed.), *Handbook of Parenting.* Mahwah, NJ: Lawrence Erlbaun, 1995.

PART IV

THE BRAIN

"How is it that little children are so intelligent and men so stupid? It must be education that does it."

—ALEXANDRE DUMAS

Cheap Trick No. 35

From the Hood to the Wood

From Mr. McGregor's cabbage patch to Winnie-the-Pooh's Hundred Acre Wood to Sesame Street, many fictional characters entertain your child. Some are funny and others are serious, but what's going on underneath? How mentally healthy are these characters? Let's start with the characters in Beatrix Potter's *The Tale of Peter Rabbit*.

Peter Rabbit has a severe impulse control problem. He never learns from experience although his cousin Benjamin Bunny repeatedly reminds him to stay away from cats. Judging from his behavior, Peter Rabbit is a glutton, a thief, and a hypochondriac, as well as greedy, emotionally immature, fearful, irresponsible, and prone to failure. He is continually disobedient and often must be sent to bed without his supper. He does not respect Mr. McGregor's property and probably suffers from some form of attention deficit disorder. He may even be a candidate for Ritalin.

Winnie-the-Pooh also suffers from attention deficit hyperactivity disorder, as well as symptoms of obsessive-compulsive disorder—constantly thinking about honey and repetitively counting over and over. If he ever leaves the Hundred Acre Wood, he would also be a prime candidate for medication, and so would some of his friends.

Poor Eeyore suffers from chronic depression and anhedonia, or in his case "an-hee-haw-donia." Piglet is filled with anxiety. Owl is dyslexic. Tigger is hyperactive and impulsive, and quite a risk-taker—he's always climbing trees and eating thistles. Finally, based on E. H. Shepard's illustrations, young Christopher Robin may be showing signs of gender identity disorder. If only he had some sort of parental figure with whom he could interact.

The *Sesame Street* characters are no better off. Big Bird suffers from delusions and hallucinations. Snuffleupagus is not just depressed; he suffers from dysthymic disorder. Perhaps of all the characters, Oscar the Grouch is most up front with his condition. He suffers from oppositional defiant disorder manifest in his negativistic, defiant, disobedient, and hostile (especially toward authority figures and celebrity guests) behaviors on the show. Finally, poor Cookie Monster might best be described as bulimic.

Think all this is silly? It is. You may doubt these "scientific" diagnoses, believing that the researchers have too much time on their hands and way too many government grants. If so...

What's the cheap psychological trick? Give your child the same benefit of the doubt. Don't be too quick to attribute his tendencies to a psychological disfuction.

REFERENCE

Rogers, J. "The 'Sesame Street' Effect: Can You Tell Me How to Get, How to Get to Crazy Street?" www.psychology.sbc.edu/bellan.htm.

Shea, S. E., K. Gordon, A. Hawkins, J. Kawchuk, and D. Smith. "Pathology in the Hundred Acre Wood: A Neurodevelopmental Perspective on A. A. Milne." *Canadian Medical Association Journal* 163 (2000): 1557–1559.

Potter, B. *The Tale of Peter Rabbit.* Lewiston, Maine: Ladybird Books, 1988.

Cheap Trick No. 36

Readin', 'Ritin', 'Rithmetic, & Ritalin

School days, rule days—and the main rule is to sit quietly in your seat and behave yourself! Then, of course, there are numerous corollaries: Do what you're told, don't annoy your neighbor, speak when you're spoken to, pay attention to your work, concentrate, don't chew gum, raise your hand to be recognized, and—the newest one—leave all weapons at home! These are a lot of rules for elementary school children to absorb and if any one rule is continually violated, some professional may label your child as hyperactive. Before you act on this, make sure you understand some of the significant differences between children and adults.

Children respond to certain common conditions very differently from adults. As a result, parents and teachers often think one thing is going on when the opposite may be the case. Take sleep, for instance.

Approximately 40 percent of all adults suffer from sleep deficit and may find themselves dozing while on the job. Children respond to a sleep deficit in the opposite way; when they're sleepy, they fight it and become more active than normal, mimicking hyperactivity. If your child is sleep deprived, he is 25 percent more likely to be diagnosed with a behavioral problem. Children (before puberty) need from 9 to 11.5 hours of uninterrupted sleep each night. Approximately 60 percent of children are sleep deficient; how many kids' alleged hyperactivity would go away if they just got enough sleep?

Problems with your child's school performance may be evidence of something other than a learning disability—he may just be overwhelmed or confused. When adults have too much work, they usually work longer hours to catch up. When younger children have difficulty or get behind in their work, they don't know what to do, so they often stop working altogether. They get bored, and they seek ways to entertain themselves. Overactivity emerges as a way to pass the time.

The same is true with unusually bright children who have already mastered material that the rest of the class finds difficult. While they're waiting for everyone else to catch up, they're doing things that may be distracting to the rest of the class.

Another more serious problem may have similar effects in your child's life. It's called childhood depression. When adults are sad, most of them act sad—they slow down, cry, or vegetate. Children act the opposite. When they're depressed, they can become behavioral problems. It's likely that there are many children out there misidentified as hyperactive when they're really depressed. Adding insult to true injury, they don't just have the wrong diagnosis, but the wrong medication as well.

There is no quick-and-easy way to deal with childhood depression; it requires professional attention. What's important, nay imperative, is the correct diagnosis. What it looks like—hyperactivity—and what it is—depression—can make it difficult to diagnose, but you must seek out a correct diagnosis. When a behavioral problem emerges, find two licensed professionals who don't know your child and don't know each other and ask each to evaluate your child. Look for professionals who are experts in child behavior—not just any Tom, Dick, and Mary from the HMO. It takes a true expert to be a child's friend.

What's the cheap psychological trick? Before accepting a diagnosis of hyperactivity, make sure your child's not sleep deprived. Also be sure he's not behind in, confused by, or bored by his schoolwork. And most importantly (and not cheap at all), get an accurate diagnosis so that if your child is suffering from depression, he will get the right treatment.

REFERENCE

Klorman, R., J. T. Brumaghim, P. A. Fitzpatrick, A. D. Borgstedt, and J. Strauss. "Clinical and Cognitive Effects of Methylphenidate on Children with Attention Deficit Disorder as a Function of Aggression/ Oppositionality and Age." *Journal of Abnormal Psychology* 103 (1994): 206–221.

Cheap Trick No. 37

"E" for Effort

It's one of life's cold hard truths. There are slackers in this world who manage to do half the work and get twice the pay. Fortunately, there is an approach that will allow your child to turn the tables. It's a stratagem that tricks the average teacher every time.

Start with two identical people doing the same job. One person does his work in record time and makes it look easy. The other person, equally capable, doesn't do as much but goes out of his way to show the effort involved in completing the job. When asked to evaluate the two employees, your supervisor, whether boss or teacher, will most likely favor the one who demonstrated more effort even if he did less work and took longer to do it.

In a perfect world, people would be evaluated exclusively on their skill and rewarded accordingly. In our world, the opposite is often true. Hard workers, even if their results are not as good, tend to be evaluated more positively than those who are skillful but don't draw attention to themselves. If your child wants to do well, he's got to show his effort. Make it look too easy, and he might go unnoticed and unappreciated.

Remember when your fourth grade teacher required you to show your math work in the margins? Your child should take this approach whenever possible and appropriate. The teacher may be impressed and might reward your child for his hard work as well as the right answer.

What's the cheap psychological trick? Don't just tell me what you did, show and tell me how hard you worked, too.

REFERENCE

Dugan, K. W. "Ability and Effort Attributions: Do They Affect How Managers Communicate Performance Feedback?" *Academy of Management Journal* 32 (1989): 87–114.

Cheap Trick No. 38

Helping Hands

When your mother said, "It's impolite to point," she was only partially right—she should have been more specific. And when your reading teacher told you to point to the words as you read aloud, she was teaching a useful technique, one that can improve your child's mental abilities. You don't just talk with your hands, you think with them, too. Gestures facilitate brain functioning—especially learning and reasoning.

Used together, hands and speech may or may not convey a point to the hearer, but they always help the speaker. In studies, a group of people was given a reasoning task, and then videotaped as they solved the problem. All used similar hand mannerisms or gestures as they worked through the problem. Even when individuals who had been blind from birth were given the same problem, they used similar hand gestures.

Want to help your child learn a foreign language? In addition to rote learning—memorizing alien phrases and repeating them over and over—teach her to use her hands to help her brain grasp the phrase. As you coach your child on the foreign words for numbers, let her repeat each new word while holding up the equivalent number of fingers. To learn a phrase like "I want soup," for example, your child could simulate drinking soup from a spoon while reciting the words.

Want to improve your child's reading speed? Then remember what every elementary school reading teacher suggests: Use your index finger as a pacer, moving it along the words in a book, never stopping, sweeping under a line of text, forcing your eyes to follow. Many speed-reading courses use this premise, recognizing the importance of brain-and-hand teamwork.

What's the cheap psychological trick? Even if your fingers do the walking, it's smart to let your hands do some of the talking. It's a wonderful way for your child to express himself and to learn at the same time.

REFERENCE
"Show Me What You're Thinking." *Psychology Today* (March/April, 1998).

Cheap Trick No. 39

A Gift or a Curse?

Every parent wants one—a gifted child, that is—but not every parent understands the requirements of a gifted child. These kids require a totally different "Owner's Manual." After you read the parenting book for regular children, you better find one specifically geared to rearing gifted children. Consider William James Sidis, a math genius who graduated from Harvard at age fifteen. Instead of using his gift, he despised it and chose menial positions in order to hide his abilities from the public. Being a gifted child isn't always a welcome gift. If you think you've got a little genius in your household, here are some things you need to know.

Athlete Artist Scientist

First, most school systems screen for gifted students using only intelligence tests. While it may be cost-effective and efficient, this approach is shortsighted at best. Intelligence tests provide one overall evaluation—the child's IQ score. Many parents (and teachers, too) assume that if a child scores well on an IQ text, her abilities are equally high in other areas. Not so. It's not unusual for a gifted child to be incredibly talented in one area yet deficient in another. Gifted children who are deficient in some areas often have difficulty understanding why and how this happens and tend to spend way too much time dwelling on their inadequacies instead of their glorious strengths. To make sure your child's gift isn't a curse, ask for a complete educational test battery—not just an IQ test. After approximately three hours of testing, your child's abilities, strengths, and weaknesses will be more clearly delineated.

Being gifted is often easier for boys than it is for girls. Academically superior boys—especially if they have any athletic ability—have little trouble maintaining popularity among their peers. Exceptionally bright girls, however, often meet with resistance from their friends. These gifted girls may underplay their abilities—even underachieve—and settle for lower grades just to be accepted.

Conventional wisdom suggests that the parents of gifted children may contribute to their children's problems because they push them too much. Overbearing stage parents may contribute to a gifted child's difficulties, but in many cases, truly gifted children also pressure themselves. Add any parental influence and the result is a child who may burn out early.

What's the cheap psychological trick? Remember giftedness can be a gift and a curse. So, praise your child, but don't push her. Celebrate her abilities and identify and address any deficiencies.

REFERENCE
Winner, E. *Gifted Children: Myths and Realities*. New York: HarperCollins, 1997.

Cheap Trick No. 40

Put Me In, Coach!

Y ou've probably wondered why your child will do anything his coach tells him to do but ignores or resists your directions and instructions. What does the coach know that you don't?

In a study of effective coaches, researchers first dissected their behavior. They looked at the ways the coaches bonded with players—as well as the quantity and types of those interactions.

The most successful coaches spent 50 percent of their coaching time instructing players on what to do and how to do it. But, you may say, I instruct my children, and they don't respond. Well, coaches are doing others things, too!

Coaches motivate. In fact, they spend approximately

15 percent of their time saying things that reinforce their instructions and motivate their players. They encourage their charges and inspire them to work even harder. These motivational comments activate and intensify previously instructed behaviors.

Researchers also found that the best coaches praise their players 15 percent of the time. Whether the praise is verbal or nonverbal is insignificant. Most individuals respond to a smile or a pat on the back just as quickly as they do to spoken praise.

These three coaching procedures—instructing, motivating, and praising—add up to roughly 80 percent. What the best coaches do with the remaining 20 percent is equally telling.

Occasionally and inevitably, players misbehave or don't perform and are subject to discipline. As a result, 15 percent of coaching time is devoted to scolding, chiding, and reprimanding players. But here's the kicker. Half of that time spent reprimanding is spent reinstructing players and demonstrating correct behavior. A good coach goes out of his way to teach the player the right thing to do rather than belaboring the inappropriate action that precipitated the scolding. Ineffective coaches just yell; effective coaches yell, remediate, and fix.

(Just in case you're curious, the remaining 5 percent of coaching time was spent on behaviors described as uncodeable—things like the ubiquitous male bonding "slap on the butt" ritual and housekeeping details.)

What's the cheap psychological trick? It's called the four-to-one rule. The most effective coaches, teachers, bosses, and even parents use it! Out of every five interactions with your child, focus on making four of them full of instruction, motivation, and praise. When you do have to scold, try to devote half of that painful time to reinstruction.

REFERENCE

Berns, R. M. *Child, Family, School, Community: Socialization and Support.* Fort Worth, TX: Harcourt Brace College Publishers, 1997.

Humphrey, J. H. *Sports for Children: A Guide for Adults.* Springfield, IL: Charles C. Thomas Publisher Ltd., 1993.

Cheap Trick No. 41

Thinker Toys

Visit any local toy store, and you'll see everything from old-fashioned to ultramodern playthings. On the average, parents select toys merely because their children want them. But parents are missing a great opportunity if that's the only way they choose toys. Thinker toys can also be used to solve a myriad of problems.

Technically, all toys are thinker toys. All toys teach something, although it may not be something you want your child to learn. Toys are powerful teachers because they offer a fun way to learn. Parents who are not in the know just give toys to their children with little thought as to what this toy is teaching them. Wise parents use toys to solve educational problems, to improve their children's minds, and to manage their children's lives. Here are some examples.

Want to improve your child's eye-to-hand abilities and his balance at the same time? Give him a yo-yo. It's a quick, inexpensive, and easy way to improve neuronal messages from the eyes to the brain and then to the hands. These skills—essential for good coordination—include many diverse actions, from hitting or catching a ball, to printing or writing cursive. Of course, working on eye-to-hand coordination can help adults, too! If you want to improve your golf game, start with a yo-yo. It'll help you keep your eye on the ball.

Want to improve your child's ability to plan and to process abstractly? Give him an Erector set. It's an easy way to improve his spatial abilities. After all, he must first see his creation in his mind (spatially) before he can create it in the real world (physically). Many contemporary toys teach the same spatial skills, but they often have extras like projectiles and guns thrown in, and they usually cost more. Model airplanes, puzzles, and even crayons—all far less expensive—can do the same thing and keep both young and old minds sharp.

Want to improve your child's self-control, patience, memory, coordination, ability to sit still, and emotional sensitivity? Give him a musical instrument. Learning a musical instrument requires all of those qualities and has another side effect as well. There is a strange, unexplained link between music, mathematics, and brain development. Music lessons can also improve math skills. (Don't forget, Einstein was a concert-quality violinist.) Too bad some school boards don't seem to know about this music-math link. If they did, music wouldn't be the first thing eliminated when budgets get tight.

What's the cheap psychological trick? All toys teach something. Toys can contain either a solution or more problems. Choose carefully and your toy gifts can be more than a "present"—they can create a "future" as well.

REFERENCE

Bodnar, J. *Dollars & Sense for Kids.* Washington, D.C.: Kiplinger Books, 1999.

Applause! Applause!

What do big leaguers and your little leaguer have in common? Maybe you've wondered what makes Tiger Woods so different from your putt-putt golfer? Or what it is that separates your little star from the Julia Robertses of the world? To paraphrase the famous question from the play, *Applause, Applause,* "What is it that they're living for?" The answer is a cheap psychological trick, one that has the power to make your little performer a star in his world or perhaps even the known universe. All it takes is an audience and a little preparation.

Professional performers have spectacular abilities, but they also have an audience. They thrive on the adoration of that audience, but they also know how to use it to their advantage. For years, social psychologists have known that an audience is far more than a group of people sitting there, watching someone perform. An audience has the power to enhance a performance or inhibit it in a way that may discourage a person from ever performing again.

From cockroaches to white rats to college sophomores, all creatures respond to an audience of their peers. When you demonstrate a talent you've mastered for others, then the energy of the audience works with you and takes you to new heights.

But preparation is equally important; performing for an audience before you're ready can backfire on you. If you show off prematurely, then the audience's negative reaction will impede your performance and cause anxiety. That feeling will probably linger with you through future performances with different audiences.

If your child is preparing for a piano recital, it's important for him to be able to play his material flawlessly. The confidence that results from this preparation will help him interact well with the audience, and he will benefit from their approval. If, however, he's unsure of his abilities, the mere presence of the audience can lead to a poor performance. The same is true of any skill your child is attempting to master.

Have you been wondering why your child is the class clown? Easy to explain. He has the ability to make people laugh. He's probably planned and practiced his material ahead of time, waiting for the right opportunity. His audience responds, he receives attention, and he enjoys it. He continues to create laughter because the audience's attention is far more energizing than any punishment doled out by the teacher.

What's the cheap psychological trick? Practice makes perfect. If your child knows what he's doing, an audience can be his best friend. If he's unprepared, an audience can do him far more harm than good.

REFERENCE

Cruz, A., and Robert Nickas (Eds.). *Performance Anxiety*. Chicago: Museum of Contemporary Art, 1997.

Your New Best Friend: The Librarian

In this complicated age, parents are conditioned to think that you need a specialist to solve a problem. That may be true in certain situations, but you don't always need to seek out professional help at the first sign of an issue with your child. There's a wealth of knowledge out there just waiting to be tapped. There are your parents—after all they reared you. Then there's your child's school. Her teachers may be spending more time with your child than you are. There's always your minister, rabbi, priest, or other religious leader. All of these folks can share with you a wealth of information on many, many subjects.

Then there's your librarian. That's right. Your librarian. Because he knows a cheap psychological trick, he may know more about rearing children than many pediatricians and psychologists.

Is your child angry with herself because she's having difficulty in math? Ask your librarian to recommend a book about a child who had the same problem. Is your little girl upset because she's not growing up as fast as her other friends? Once again, another book to the rescue. What about a relative going off to war? Or the facts of life? Or taking care of a puppy? In almost every case, you can find a book to address the issue. This cheap psychological trick called "bibliotherapy" works like a charm.

Here's how to make this work for you. First, tell the librarian about your child's problem. Ask him to direct you to a book that's age appropriate for your child and that focuses on this problem. Your librarian will be able to recommend a book that may help your child with his problem.

One additional trick: In most libraries, you can find a remarkable book called *Bookfinder*. This index of books by age, subject, and title can help you locate a book that may help you and your child. If your child is having trouble with puberty, simply look up that topic and select something appropriate from the list of summarized books.

What's the cheap psychological trick? You can learn a lot from a librarian. You can learn even more from books. The librarian is a wonderful resource to help you match problem, book, and solution. Of course, you could use the internet, but it's not as warm and fuzzy as a librarian's touch.

REFERENCE

Dreyer, S. *Bookfinder: A Guide to Children's Literature About the Needs and Problems of Youth Aged 2–15.* Circle Pines, Minnesota: American Guidance Service, 1977.

Cheap Trick No. 44

The Mind's Eye

There are thousands of technical and scientific articles published throughout the world each day, and that doesn't count those published electronically. More than 1,000 new manuscripts arrive for cataloging at the United States Library of Congress every twenty-four hours. It's a logical question to ask: Is it possible for your child to absorb all the information that's thrown at him? There is one cheap psychological trick that can help. It's a trick that the best elementary school teachers use daily. They tell their students, "Don't just say the word, see a picture of it in your head," or "As you read, watch the story unfold in your mind's eye." Researchers have known for years that it's easier to remember a picture than it is to remember a word—and the applications are legion.

If you want your child to get more out of what she reads and remember it long after, teach her this approach. Don't just read the words—visualize what you're reading as a movie in your head. Say the words to yourself while watching the action in your head. Doing so activates the mind's eye and the reading centers in your brain, but it doesn't stop there. As you're watching the movie unfold before your very eyes, the emotional parts of the brain are engaged as well. So now this one passage has involved three separate parts of the brain, and you've tripled the chances you'll remember what you read.

If you're helping your child learn a new language, try this same technique. Many people hear a new foreign word and translate it in their head into their mother tongue. That's the rote method, and it's not as efficient as visualizing the object while repeating the foreign word and associating that image with the foreign word.

Want to teach your child how to study smart rather than long? As she reads about George Washington cross-ing the Delaware, she should try to see him doing just that. What's he wearing? Who's in the boat with him? What's the date on the calendar? Anything she can turn into a picture will facilitate her remembering it and even enjoying it.

Most children are pre-wired with an ability to learn via visualization. When they're young, it's often the preferred approach to learning. As they get older, however, they sometimes relegate the ability to see what they read to the back seat. Encourage them to hang on to that skill.

What's the cheap psychological trick? Picture it, and it makes more sense.

REFERENCE

Dr. Buff's second-grade teacher, Miss Pilkenton.

Norton, D. E. *Through the Eyes of a Child: An Introduction to Children's Literature* (4th ed.). New York: Macmillan, 1995.

Handwriting on the Wall

Parents are excited when their children learn how to form their letters. The act of writing involves fine motor skills that can be affected by any number of things. Many an expert has reminded teachers and mental health professionals about the relationship between children's behavior and their handwriting.

Parents need not worry just because their children's handwriting is difficult to read or illegible. As long as it stays *consistently* illegible, poor handwriting doesn't usually signal a problem. But parents should be alert if they notice a *drastic* change in their child's handwriting. A sudden change can signal anything from emotional pain to even some physical problems.

But what if your child's handwriting is just plain

messy? There's a cheap psychological trick you can employ. It's called a fountain pen.

Once upon a time—in a kindler, gentler, less technological time—every child had to master the fountain pen. It was standard educational practice for that time, but those days are long gone. That's unfortunate, because fountain pens can be useful. A fountain pen works wonders on increasing a child's hand-to-eye coordination. Shaping words by hand and learning how to express herself with a grown-up fountain pen can instill in your child a love of handwritten communication. In this day of e-mail, when many of the social graces seem to be dwindling, this will teach your child both the gentle art of penmanship and the love of the written word.

What's the cheap psychological trick? If a child's handwriting changes suddenly, check out what's going on in her world. And if you'd like for your child to improve her handwriting and learn to love written communication, give her a fountain pen. But one word to the wise: Make sure her first fountain pen is full of washable, non-permanent ink.

REFERENCE

Silver, L. B. *The Misunderstood Child: A Guide for Parents of Children with Learning Disabilties* (2nd ed.). New York: Tab Books, 1992.

Cheap Trick No. 46

The Big Hand Says

Awatch is a special gift that marks time in so many ways and one of the finest presents you can give your child. But be careful. You may think that a digital watch is the perfect gift, but actually, it's not. Instead, buy your child an analog watch—one that comes with its own cheap psychological trick.

An analog watch is far superior to a digital watch when it comes to learning how to tell time. A digital watch—one that shows the time numerically—is a no-brainer. If your child has learned his numbers, he can simply look at it and tell time. But an analog watch—one with hands—teaches the entire concept of time. As your child learns how long it takes the hands to move, he spatially and intuitively learns how much time is used up in that interval.

Before bedtime, your child probably begs, "Just let me stay up five more minutes." Typically, children don't know how long five minutes actually is. With an analog watch, however, he'll begin to learn that five minutes is the time it takes the little hand to move from one big number to the next.

An analog watch is also a wonderful way to speed up your child every morning. As the child begins to master the movements of the watch's hands, he or she truly begins to understand what's really meant when you say, "Hurry up! We only have fifteen minutes before we gotta leave for school."

W**hat's the cheap psychological trick?** Knowing how to tell time is a good thing, but understanding it is far better. An analog wristwatch accomplishes both feats with time to spare.

REFERENCE

Older, J., and M. Halsey. *Telling Time: How to Tell Time on Digital and Analog Clocks.* Watertown, MA: Charlesbridge Publishing, 2000.

Cheap Trick No. 47

You Can Do It!

This is one of those cheap tricks that's pure common sense. Everyone knows about it; but in a peculiar quirk of human logic, few continue to use it. Many parents actively use this trick on small children, yet when their children hit puberty, they seem to forget about it. Too bad. This is a parenting trick that works at all ages.

Parents who regularly say to their child "You can do it!" rear children who tend to achieve more throughout their lifetime. This encouragement has a technical name. It's called a "self-efficacy expectation," and it's sort of a cross between the Little Engine That Could's credo and pop psychology's affirmations. No matter. It works quite well as a motivational strategy.

Do you want your child to do well on a test? Encourage her to study, but don't stop there. On exam day, say, "Good luck. I know you can do it." Some researchers have found that just the simple act of saying "Good luck" can raise expectations and the desire to do well. Then teach your child to say silently to herself as she starts the test, "I can do this."

What's the cheap psychological trick? Regularly say to your child, "You can do this." Then teach your child to repeat to herself "I can do this" before any difficult task. If it worked for the Little Engine That Could, it can work for your child.

REFERENCE

Bandura, A. *Social Foundations of Thought and Action: A Social-Cognitive Theory.* Englewood Cliffs, NJ: Prentice-Hall, 1986.

Cheap Trick No. 48

The Little Engine That Did

Remember Watty Piper's book called *The Little Engine That Could?* The train had a choice—to succeed or fail. She thought she could succeed, but she wasn't sure. Throughout the story, she gave herself a pep talk: "I think I can. I think I can." Finally, the "I think I can" turned into "I thought I could." "I don't think I can" never crept into her pep talk; if it had, her brain would have taken over, and she never would have made it over the mountain.

It's important to teach your child the Little Engine's positive approach. Otherwise, failure is quite likely, thanks to his brain. When the thought of failure first occurs, the brain vetoes any previous strategy to achieve success within four-tenths of a second. But it doesn't stop there. Within four-tenths of a second, the brain vetoes any strategy that might ensure success, followed two-tenths of a second later with actions that create and assure failure. Think "I don't think I can" enough, and you won't be able to do anything.

Now back to the Little Engine. She never allowed the fear of failure to creep in; instead she repeatedly affirmed, "I think I can. I think I can." Teach your child to follow her example; within four-tenths of a second, a strategy to achieve success will occur to him, followed two-tenths of a second later with positive actions.

What's the cheap psychological trick? Don't dismiss this approach as pop psychology. It takes the same amount of energy to think about success as it does to think about failure. Negative or positive thinking appears to be a learned preference—even learned by the age three. So, the next time your child says, "I don't think I can do this," let your response be, "I think you can, and I'll show you how." Then when he succeeds, respond, "I knew you could."

REFERENCE

Piper, W. *The Little Engine That Could.* New York: Grosset & Dunlap, 1978.

Goodkin, K. and A. P. Visser (Eds.). *Psychoneuroimmunology: Stress, Mental Disorders, and Health.* Washington, D.C.: American Psychiatric Press, 2000.

PART V

THE HEART

"We find a delight in the beauty and happiness of children that makes the heart too big for the body."

—RALPH WALDO EMERSON

Cheap Trick No. 49

Don't Read This!

If you've ever wondered where your child learned her negative attitude, you might want to take a look in the mirror. If you want to know where she learned many of her positive attitudes, take another look in that mirror. You receive credit for both the negative and the positive. So here's the deal. If you want to help your child have a positive attitude, you must accentuate the positive and eliminate the negative. It's not as tough as it sounds. What you say matters, but what you do not say is actually more important. For instance, have you ever said any of the following to your child?

♡ "Take this glass of milk and do *not* spill it."

♡ "Do *not* slam the door."

♡ "Study hard and do *not* fail the test."

Invariably after you say such things, the milk spills, the door slams, and the child fails the test.

A young child who hears you tell her *not* to spill her milk tries to mentally process what you've said. In order to do so, she must visualize the scenario you've suggested, including the negative outcome. Once she's seen the milk spilled, the door slammed, and the test failed, those outcomes are practically inevitable.

To prove this point, try this experiment. Here goes, just do as you're asked:

♡ Do *not* think of a white horse.

Even as you were reading the sentence, you saw a white horse. Then you had to try and not think about that white horse, perhaps by changing it to an appaloosa or a dapple gray. Even you couldn't avoid thinking of the white horse first, and you're an adult. Your child doesn't know how to take the second step of transforming the image; her brain cells stall on the negative image you've presented to her.

Now take a look at those sentences reworded in a more proactive, educative manner. Each creates a positive mental picture of the action you're trying to achieve in your child.

♡ "Take this glass of milk and hold it with both hands."

♡ "Close the door gently, please."

♡ "Study hard and do well on your quiz."

What's the cheap psychological trick? If you want to teach your child to get positive results, make sure to accentuate the positive in what you say to her. What you say is important, but what you *don't* say has more of an effect on your child's behavior.

REFERENCE

Wegner, D. M., D. J. Schneider, S. Carter, and T. White. "Paradoxical Effects of Thought Suppression." *Journal of Personality and Social Psychology* 53 (1987): 5–13.

Social Security

First, the truth. People never give up their security blankets. They just trade them in for more adult-appropriate objects as they age. In fact, some human behavior researchers speculate that given current pressured work conditions, more and more security objects (four-leaf clovers, rabbit's feet, lucky pennies) are finding their way into the workplace. Just like your child with her favorite teddy, those adults feel safer and more secure when they have a little talisman nearby.

And after reviewing the science involved, you'll realize that a security object is a bit more sophisticated than it appears to be—and you'll understand why your child holds on to her favorite teddy.

Everyone has people and things they care deeply about. We can develop caring attachments early to such things as a stuffed animal or a real pet. Things we care about at an early age that give us a sense of safety and security are called "transitional objects." A survey once assessed the prevalence of these simple attachments (e.g., dolls, teddy bears, fuzzy caps, "billy-doats," blankets, stuffed animals, even diapers) used early in life. Researchers found that 88 percent of girls and 71 percent of boys who participated in the survey had at least one special something.

It appears that these "woobies" and "blankies" are the tools that teach children how to care for people, places, and other things. In other words, when they attach to their "billy-doats," they start to learn what it's like to care for, to take care of, and to love things outside themselves. This inclination should be encouraged in both little boys and girls.

What's the cheap psychological trick? If you care enough, encourage your child to attach to a security object, and don't be so quick to take it away. You may be indirectly teaching your child how to take care of you when you grow old!

REFERENCE

Melson, G. F., and A. Fogel. "Learning to Care." *Psychology Today* 22 (January, 1988): 39–45.

Shafii, T. "The Prevalence and Use of Transitional Objects: A Study of 230 Adolescents." *Journal of American Academy of Child Psychiatry* 25 (November, 1986): 805–808.

Big Boys Don't Cry?

It was that famous group of philosophers, The Four Seasons, who admonished that "Big Girls Don't Cry." The truth is, girls are allowed to cry, even in public. The song might have been more aptly named "Big Boys Don't Cry," since they are the ones who are discouraged from doing so! Many parents teach little boys not to cry, except on rare occasions, because they think it is weak and inappropriate.

Social scientists agree that there are only two times when men are allowed to cry without being perceived as weak. The first occasion—the death of a loved one—makes sense; but you'll never guess the second. Men are permitted to weep freely, but not excessively, at the loss of a major athletic competition. It's unfortunate that men are limited to these two occasions, because if little boys were allowed to cry, they just might live as long as women. Take a look at this garden-variety experiment.

Mr. Jones cuts up one onion. When he cries, he collects his tears and dries his eyes. Then he thinks about a sad event. When he weeps, he collects his tears. He sends these two samples away to a lab. He will find out that the tears from these two situations are chemically different. Tears from onions are a watery, saline solution, whose purpose is to clean the eyes of pollutants. Tears from sad events are chock full of rich chemicals designed to wash away pain. Crying is a healthy safety valve, so you might as well take advantage of this truly cheap psychological trick, especially if you're under the weather.

Say you're home suffering from a first-class stopped-up nose. Crying may help you heal faster. Laboratory rats have proved this point. Researchers have surgically wounded rats and then induced rat tears via a liquid irritant. Result: The rats that cried healed faster. So when you're sitting home feeling sorry for yourself, tear up, and you might get back to work faster.

Here's an easy way to turn a ninety-pound weakling into a more manly man—and to make the manly man more sensitive. Researchers have found that crying mellows overly masculine men, but it makes effeminate men more masculine. It's a testosterone thing. If your testosterone levels are high, they'll drop after an extended crying jag! These tearful men will find themselves feeling much less aggressive and driven. If your testosterone levels are low, after you dry your eyes, you'll be ready to kick sand in someone's face. You'll feel more aggressive, and your measured testosterone level, now increased, will prove it!

If you want your child to be well rounded and happy, make sure he learns that it's okay to cry. Start with the classic movies and books from your own childhood. Recall those wonderfully sad stories like *Old Yeller* or *Charlotte's Web*. These tried and true classics will teach your child how to express sadness and deal effectively with pain. Learning how to do so at an early age—with family members present for comfort and support—may be just what your child needs to combat and to reduce the impact of today's movies steeped in exaggerated violence, bloody aggression, and little human emotion.

What's the cheap psychological trick? Make sure your children, particularly boys, learn that crying is a natural and even healing response. From the first birth cry to adult mourning, shedding tears is a human safety valve and a built-in device that releases conflict, tension, and pain. Little boys do cry, and big boys should, too.

REFERENCE

Fox, J. L. "Crying Mellows Some, Masculinizes Others." *Psychology Today* 19 (1985): 14.

Nighty Night, Nightmares

"Now I lay me down to sleep..." At bedtime, you hope for a quiet night and sweet dreams for your children. Unfortunately, that's not always the case. Sometimes children have nightmares. How you handle the situation can contribute to your child's positive sleep experiences—not just for the next few nights, but for your young one's lifetime.

First off, nightmares are few and far between. Some researchers suggest that children (and adults, too) typically experience only two nightmares a year. If your child is having more nightmares than you think is normal, here's a cheap psychological trick you might like to try.

The morning after your child has a nightmare, ask him to tell you about his bad dream. Something like this should do the trick: "I've had bad dreams before. What did you dream about?" And off he'll go, telling you about the monsters that were attacking him. Your job is to listen for themes of helplessness. When you hear one, here's what you do. Say to your child, "Wow! He was really chasing you. What could you do to protect yourself?" Then your child might say something like, "Take out my slingshot and protect myself," or "Call 9-1-1," or "Call for you." You can even say to your child, "Let's pretend we're dreaming right now, and let's fix that mean old monster." This technique teaches your child that he's capable of protecting himself. That will help while he's awake and asleep; the brain sometimes has difficulty distinguishing the difference.

You may even be able to take a preventative measure. It's possible to manipulate a dream through a technique called lucid dreaming. If you want to teach your child this technique, try this. Say to your child, "Sweetie, tonight, if you dream that dream again, make sure you punch the monster in the nose." Before your child goes to sleep tonight, ask him to pause and think to himself, "Whatever I dream, I can control." During a dream, once he realizes that he is dreaming, he can direct the action of that dream in a way he likes. It's not magic, just another ability of the incredible human brain.

One type of nightmare scares parents more than children. Night terrors *(pavor nocturnus)* are rare, but a few children have them as often as three or four times a month. Night terrors occur at a different stage of sleep from dream sleep. They typically start with the sleeping child emitting a blood-curdling scream. She may be found sitting up in bed or even running around, greatly agitated. Since the child is disoriented, she may not recognize her parents. Fortunately, the attack usually subsides after a few minutes, and the child drops off to sleep, remembering nothing. It's very difficult to wake a child during night terrors; but if you can, the attack will end. The good news is that your child will rarely remember night terrors, and fortunately, most children outgrow this condition. If they persist, however, professional assistance is in order.

What's the cheap psychological trick? Most nightmares are like vaccines. They're painful, but they can also be beneficial. The good news is that they can be controlled, and you can teach your child how. In fact, you may even learn how yourself!

REFERENCE

Bakwin, H., and R. M. Bakwin. *Behavior Disorders in Children.* Philadelphia: W. B. Saunders Company, 1972.

Kiss Her, Dad!

It's a common scene at airport, train, and bus stations: Family members waiting for a parent to arrive home from a trip. Just the other day, a mom and her five-year-old son were patiently waiting for dad to arrive on his flight. They were excited. As fate would have it, the flight was delayed, but their enthusiasm was undaunted. Finally, the father arrived, and the little boy ran up and gave him one of those I've-really-missed-you hugs. Then the father walked over to the mother and embraced her as well. The little boy, watching all the while, tugged on his father's trousers and said, "Go ahead, Dad! Kiss her!" What did the little boy know that his father didn't?

It has almost become trite to remind parents that

they are role models for their children. The technical term is "observational learning"; children learn from watching adult behaviors, and they model the behaviors they see. This time, put aside the obvious—the fact that children learn how to behave from watching adults—and look a little deeper. Here's what happens when a child sees his parents being affectionate with each other.

Children are constantly looking for proof that their parents love each other. In a child's mind, this is tantamount to security, safety, and protection. When a child sees his parents being affectionate with each other, he realizes that his family is intact and secure. Children pay far more attention to adult behaviors than to adult words. In addition, your affectionate behavior toward your spouse is indirectly training your child how to respond to his future spouse.

What's the cheap psychological trick? Show your affection to your spouse in front of your children. All will be happier and feel more secure. The love you display today will teach your children how to treat their own families when they are adults.

REFERENCE

Bandura, A. *Social Learning Theory*. Englewood Cliffs, NJ: Prentice Hall, 1977.

Love Me Tender

Somewhere in the course of the ubiquitous bird and bees talk, a child will ask, "How will I know if I'm really in love?" Easy to ask, hard to answer. A scientific explanation is in order.

The laws of complementarity tell us that when you're in love, you put your best foot forward; your attraction to another brings out the best in you. On the flip side, disdain for another brings out the worst in you. So, to find out how real your child's love is, ask him, "Does this person bring out the best in you?" If the answer is affirmative, his feelings are likely to be real.

Does your child have a crush on his teacher? A crush like this usually serves a valuable purpose. Any child who lives to please his teacher will turn his homework in on time, spend more time studying, and maybe even improve his hygiene. Don't worry—while crushes tend to end by about fifth grade, the love of learning engendered by that humble crush can last a lifetime. In this scenario, your child's crush on his teacher brings out the best in him.

So, when your child says to you, "How do I know if I'm in love?" you can answer, "Well, if this person brings out the best in you, then it's probably love." As the conversation progresses, you can throw in, " If they don't, then that's just a physical attraction."

What's the cheap psychological trick? Teach your child to look to his own responses to determine whether or not he's really in love.

REFERENCE

Dryer, D. C., and L. M. Horowitz. "When Do Opposites Attract? Interpersonal Complementarity Versus Similarity." *Journal of Personality and Social Psychology* 72 (1997): 592–603.

Tricks That Treat

It was a dark and stormy night—the spirits were afoot. Howling winds, thundering rains, stupefying lightning—yet, somehow, there was an eerie silence inside this Gothic mansion, which magnified the slightest sound, rendering it explosive. So alone, so very alone—not a living soul in sight; cries for help would go unheard, unanswered, and unknown. Only one small candle lighted the cavernous room. So dark, so very dark; nothing was visible beyond the flickering flame. Yet the shadows were alive, and every innocent movement was proof positive that it was the perfect night for death. And no doubt one blood-curdling murder, by knife, will happen before this night is o'er. Be afraid. Be very afraid.

Bet that story got your attention; and if you take a good look at it, you'll notice that it's rather simple. But what is it that makes this story so scary? It's full of cheap psychological tricks—ones you can use to tell a scary story over a campfire or at Halloween—ones that create fear and tremblings in your little listeners. Not to worry. Learning how to deal with fear at an early age is actually good for your child. And children love a scary story, just make sure your child's old enough to listen.

Trick No. 1—It's gotta be dark! Humans learn to be afraid of the dark early on. This fear tends to "go away"—although not completely—around adolescence and then rear its ugly head toward middle age. But what makes this "dark device" work for any horror writer is that it creates the sense of alone-ness and vulnerability. When one's in the dark it's only human nature to make the situation worse than it really is and blow it out of proportion. This holds whether one is physically in the dark or mentally in the dark concerning an unknown future. Just the use of the word "dark" causes the eyes to open wide in an attempt to take in more light. Murders that happen in the daylight are just as deadly as murders that happen at night, but the night makes it seem worse.

Trick No. 2—It's gotta be loud. This doesn't mean that the story is told in a loud voice, but rather told using accentuated words like "crashing," "thundering," and "stupifying." When these words are punctuated, they catch the listener off guard. Humans are born with a protection device—the fear of loud noises. Use words that evoke loud, punctuating sounds, and your story will touch a truly primal fear.

Trick No. 3— It's gotta have ordinary, gar- den-variety fears which the listener experi- ences in real life. Everyday dangers are better than natural catastrophes, stock market crashes, computer glitches, airplane crashes, nuclear disasters, and wars. Granted these are all hair-raising events, but in a Halloween story they just don't have the same thrill as snakes, rats, deep water, heights, and the all-time favorite horror

It was dark and scary...

story gimmick, knives. When you see the shiver go up their spine, you'll know you picked the right fear.

Trick No. 4—It's gotta have some disgusting stuff. When adults hear "disgusting stuff," they tend to turn off, but when kids hear about worms oozing from dead flesh, ooey-gooey sticky body organs, or strange foods, it gets their fearful juices going. Recall the feast scene in the movie, "Indiana Jones and the Temple of Doom." The foods served—eyeballs, live baby eels, monkey brains—evoked the fear gag reflex. One little warning: Make sure that the "disgusting things" you select for children are age appropriate, or you'll need more than a night-light at bedtime.

Trick No. 5—Finally, once you grab the listeners, reel 'em in. Whether you're telling a joke or a horror story, watch the listener's body language. In anticipation of the punch line, there is a tightening of body muscles, a leaning forward, and an intense gazing, fixed on the storyteller. When you see these signs, end the story with a really loud "Boo!" Every camp counselor has told the story of the man who stalks the world, searching for his missing golden arm. "Who has my golden arm?" he repeats in a spooky voice. When the kids are sufficiently into the story—tightening, leaning, and gazing—the camp counselor turns to one unsuspecting camper, grabs him, and loudly declares, "It's you!" This catching off guard, scaring even, releases the built-up tension in screams. It's that simple, and every horror movie uses that as its main ploy.

What's the cheap psychological trick? Kids love scary stories. At the right time, right moment, and the right age (not too young and not too old), a scary story is a wonderful device that can bond parent and child and teach a child how to deal with fears.

REFERENCE

Rozin, P., and A. Fallon. "That's Disgusting." *Psychology Today 19* (July 1985): 60–63.

Cheap Trick No. 56

Close Encounters

Every child wants a picture taken with Santa. After all, the jolly old fellow is supposed to be lovable, affable, and agreeable. All the child has to do is climb upon Santa's lap, ask for her fondest desire, and she might find it waiting for her on Christmas morning. And so the good little boys and girls patiently stand in line, rehearse their requests, and wait for their moment with Old St. Nick. Then one child goes ballistic—screams at the top of his lungs, refuses to meet Santa, and must be taken away to calm down. Too bad his parents didn't know a cheap psychological trick, one designed to work long before the face-to-face meeting with Father Christmas.

It's called "distance before familiarity," or DBF. Humans tend to like things to which they're exposed over time. Brief exposures and slow movements toward the object reduce fear and create an atmosphere of familiarity. In the case of Santa, here's how it works.

Children are taught to be afraid of strangers. When a parent plops her child right in Santa's lap, the screaming and clinging that often results is just the child doing what her brain thinks is best for her own protection. Smart parents invoke the distance-before-familiarity rule.

Before the big day with Santa, go to the mall and allow your child to stand back and watch. At home, let Dad pretend to be Santa; give the child, in advance, a chance to perceive Santa's life-size proportions. Make sure Dad does the whole routine: The "Ho-Ho-Ho's" and the "Have you been a good little boy and girl?" questions. Three experiences before the big day should prepare your child for meeting the big guy in the red suit.

What's the cheap psychological trick? It doesn't matter if it's Santa, the new pediatrician, or Mickey Mouse; using the distance-before-familiarity technique helps everyone adjust—even adults.

REFERENCE

Copjec, J., and M. Sorkin (Eds.). *Giving Ground: The Politics of Propinquity.* London: Verso Books, 1999.

Cheap Trick No. 57

Sick Days

L ots of books offer tips on entertaining your child when he's home sick. This time it's *you,* not your child. Occasionally, you may find yourself with more than a tummy ache, and a trip to the hospital is in order. If you handle this situation correctly, you can teach your child a valuable lesson.

First, it doesn't matter whether it's a bad cold or a life-threatening illness, honesty is the best policy—but don't go overboard. Make sure that all children in the household are kept informed, but don't give your children more information than they can understand and tell them only in small doses. Too much information about an ill parent can be overwhelming and can result in all sorts of problems in other areas, notably school.

Even if you are confined to the hospital for a while, discuss with your spouse or the caregiver ways to maintain the child's daily routine. That means: Bedtime and meals at the same time as always. This is an incredibly important point. In a child's life, routine is the most important thing after a parent's love; in fact they may be synonymous in some ways. As the child is adjusting to a parent's illness, even the slightest deviation in routine can be upsetting.

Finally, let your child become involved in caring for you. If possible, find ways for him to help you as you recover.

What's the cheap psychological trick? Let your child see what's going on, and he won't have the need to use his imagination to envision something even worse. When he knows what's going on, he also knows he's a valued member of the family. And most important of all, this experience can teach caring.

REFERENCE

Garber, S. W., M. D. Garber, and R. Spizman. *Good Behavior*. New York: Villard Books, 1987.

Happy New Year!

You can learn a lot from a kid! Take New Year's resolutions, for instance. Just like adults, many kids make New Year's resolutions. Out of every five resolutions made by an average child, four will have the same theme as adult resolutions. But children tend to add a fifth resolution, and one that reveals a cheap psychological trick even the best parent should remember, practice, and encourage.

Approximately 50 percent of the population, children included, make the following four types of resolutions:

Resolution #1—Improve nasty habits. Just like adults, children know their bad habits are unacceptable. As a result, many children resolve to stop biting their fingernails or pulling their hair.

Resolution #2—Improve work. Just like adults, children want to do better at their work, which for them means school. As a result, they want to study harder, make better grades, and learn more.

Resolution #3—Improve relationships with friends. Adults and children alike resolve to get along with their peers.

Resolution #4—Improve health. Both adults and children resolve to become healthier—eat better, lose weight, exercise more—during the upcoming year.

But it's the fifth New Year's resolution that separates the children from the adults. When kids share this resolution with their parents, the adults realize that this one is the best of all.

Resolution #5—Improve behavior. When children make this fifth resolution, they usually add a quasi-prayer. It's not unusual at all for children to want to be more spiritual, although they may not know the word or exact phrase. Children tend to equate good behavior and godliness. So, when they want to be good, they're actually embracing the origins of the word "good" which comes from "God-like."

What's the cheap psychological trick? Listen to your child's resolutions and help her reach her goals. But pay even closer attention when your child spontaneously adds spirituality to her list. This is your opportunity to understand your child's current ethics, show her how to develop her spirituality, and encourage her to achieve this resolution. From the faith of a child, the seeds of a happy new year can grow.

REFERENCE

Benson, P., M. Donahue, and J. Erickson. "Adolescence and Religion: Review of the Literature from 1970–1986." *Research in the Social Scientific Study of Religion* 1 (1989): 153–181.

Cheap Trick No. 59

Your Child's Special Day

When a kid has a birthday, it's cause for celebration. In fact, maybe it's time to start a new family tradition. Check out these guidelines:

Rule 1—Don't just celebrate for a day; celebrate your child's birthday for a week. Maybe even give her a little gift every day with a big gift on the actual anniversary of her birth.

Rule 2—Take the day off; don't work on your child's birthday. Even if your child's in school, she will know you're home working on something special and that she will have your undivided attention when the school day is over. Try to take your child's entire birthday off because if you don't, demands at work may cause you to be late for the festivities.

Rule 3—If your child's birthday falls around a gift-giving holiday like Christmas, make sure she receives at least two gifts—one for the holiday and one *wrapped in birthday paper* for her birthday.

Rule 4—On your child's birthday, let her eat cake—let the whole family! On this day, the entire family is encouraged to ignore calorie counting and do fun and silly things, as long as you do them together.

Rule 5—Within reason, your child should control her environment as much as possible during her birthday week. Allowing her to make decisions—what to eat, where to go, how to celebrate—only makes the day more special.

What's the cheap psychological trick? Celebrating a child's birthday celebrates the child—there is no nobler parenting task. She'll understand that a birthday is significant to the whole family, not just to her.

REFERENCE

Sampson, A., and S. Sampson. *The Oxford Book of Ages.* New York: Oxford University Press, 1985.

Cheap Trick No. 60

Another Brick in the Wall

If you've talked to a "typical" teenager lately, no doubt you've felt as if you're beating your head against a brick wall. And, in some ways, you are. Some people say talking to a teenager is like filling a leaking tire with air. The harder you blow, the flatter it gets. Others say talking to teenagers is like being on a seesaw with an elephant; no matter how much force you exert, they don't budge. It's time you knew the truth. Your teenager is pulling a cheap psychological trick on you, and you might as well face up to the fact that it will get you every time.

In a typical conversation with another adult, we tend to mirror the other person we're speaking with. If he expresses happiness, we reflect that emotion. When we're with someone who's sad, we turn off our smile and empathize with her via somber words and a face to match. When we're talking with someone who's in an emotional frenzy, we may not match her emotion, but we tend to escalate our own behavior or at least show a similar, but lower-key emotion. It just doesn't work that way with adolescents, but we act as if it should.

Imagine you are a typical parent talking to your teenager. You say something, and she's underwhelmed at best. You escalate both emotion and volume. You find yourself getting involved in the conversation; you're doing everything you can to rouse some spark of interest, and she comes back every time underwhelmed. No matter how hard you try to make your point in your best stentorian English, no matter how emotional you get, she just kind of looks at you with that "whatever" look.

Stop explaining—you might as well stop now. Save your breath. Express yourself behaviorally. Just say to your child, "Do (fill in the blank), or lose your (fill in the blank)." The reverse also works: "When you do (fill in the blank), then you get (fill in the blank). And when your adolescent comes back at you with an emotional approach—one that has always gotten you to change your mind in the past—just mirror her usual uninvolved, flat emotion from the last encounter and give her the "whatever" look.

What's the cheap psychological trick? Your teenager knows that the calmer and more uninterested she acts, the more agitated you'll become. So, want to get a teenager's attention? Reverse your usual approach.

REFERENCE

Steinberg, L. "Reciprocal Relation between Parent-Child Distance and Pubertal Maturation. *Developmental Psychology* 24 (1988): 122–128.

Steinberg, L., J. Elmen, and N. Mounts. "Authoritative Parenting, Psychosocial Maturity and Academic Success among Adolescents." *Child Development* 60 (1988): 1424–1436.

Cheap Trick No. 61

The Silly System

As a parent, you've probably wondered why your child cries to stay with grandma or grandpa. Chances are that it's those "three little words." Grandma, grandpa, and special aunts and uncles are not as caught up in routine and remember to say, "I love you" regularly. Those are three words that children live for and parents take for granted. Parents assume that their children know that they love them. Their children probably do know this, but that doesn't mitigate the child's desire to hear those three words—often.

What can you do to make sure you remember to tell your children you love them? Be SILLY. Remember the acronym SILY; it stands for: "Say I Love You." Here are the rules:

♡ Say "I love you" as often as you think of it.

♡ Make a habit of saying it at the beginning of the day and the end of the day.

♡ Feel free to embellish the sentiment with phrases like: "I love you millions and billions." "Do you know how much I love you?" or "Could I love anyone more than you?"

♡ Express your love physically as well as verbally.

♡ Go ahead and ask your child if he loves you. It is permissible.

♡ When a child asks, "Do you love me?" stop whatever you're doing and tell them you do.

♡ If it embarrasses you, or if you can't remember to say, "I love you" or if your child is at that age when she doesn't want her friends to hear you say it, take a stickie-note, write "ILY" on it, and put it in her lunchbox or book bag.

♡ Let your children hear you tell your spouse "I love you," too.

What's the cheap psychological trick? To paraphrase Dolly G. Levi of *Hello, Dolly:* "Love is like fertilizer. It's no good until it's spread around." Crude but very true. Remember to teach this to your child at an early age. If you do, you'll hear it all through their adolescence and into adulthood and see it taught to your grandchildren.

REFERENCE

Zullo, A., and K. Zullo. *The Nanas and the Papas: A Boomer's Guide to Grandparenting.* Kansas City, MO: Andrews-McMeel Publishing, 1998.

Cheap Trick No. 62

The Number One Predictor

Underlying every question that parents ask is one central theme. Whether a parent is asking about discipline, schooling, or extracurricular activities, parents want what's best for their child, and they desire to do those things that will facilitate their offspring's success. So, let's ask the question: What is the number one predictor of any child's success?

Would you say it's the school system? Important, but not the best predictor.

What about a drug-free environment? It would be wonderful, but frankly it's unobtainable. And, it's not the number one predictor either.

What about extracurricular activities like sports, scouting, music, or drama? Nope. Not even close.

What about the church? Once again, important, but not number one.

What is the number one predictor of your child's success? You. The parent. It's those little things parents do, like being there, talking to their children, encouraging them, advising them, feeding them, disciplining them, and, of course, loving them. Throw in a good school, strong faith, and socialization skills learned through extracurricular activities, and you've got a special child.

What's the cheap psychological trick? Parents are the most important piece of the parenting puzzle.

REFERENCE

Barton, P., and R. Coley. *America's Smallest School: The Family.* Princeton, NJ: Educational Testing Services, 1992.

About the Author

Perry Buffington, Ph.D., is a psychologist, author, lecturer, and media personality. His Cheap Psychological Tricks are nationally syndicated on radio and in print. His seminars on creativity, leadership, and charisma have received international attention. Buffington is the author of hundreds of articles and numerous books, including CHEAP PSYCHOLOGICAL TRICKS, CHEAP PSYCHOLOGICAL TRICKS FOR LOVERS, and ARCHIVAL ATLANTA. He lives on Amelia Island, Florida. His web address is www.drbuff.com.

About the Illustrator

Jen Singh grew up in St. Joseph, Michigan, and studied illustration at Kendall College of Art & Design in Grand Rapids. After graduation, she moved to Atlanta, Georgia, where she has worked as an artist ever since. She also illustrated CHEAP PSYCHOLOGICAL TRICKS FOR LOVERS. Singh lives in Decatur, Georgia, with husband J. T. and her two cats.